What others are saying

Nine out of ten doctors recommend eating more bananas. But I recommend *Writing with Banana Peels*. It's packed with a complete day's supply of tips to make you a better writer.
> **Tim Bete**, former director of the Erma Bombeck Writers' Workshop and author of *Guide to Pirate Parenting*
> www.timbete.com

Banana peels reduce the appearance of wrinkles, treat headache, soothe skin after bug bites, remove warts, control acne—and now cause you to write with humor! *Writing with Banana Peels* causes outbursts of laughter right from the copyright page on! It's loaded with hilarious examples and great tips and tricks for writing with humor. From ridding warts to writing funny, you can't go wrong with banana peels.
> **Twila Belk**, writer, speaker, conference director, and leading authority on banana peels
> www.gottatellsomebody.com

I was just going to skim the publisher's review copy of Jim's book, but ended up reading the whole thing. It was excellent, and I laughed out loud several times. By giving specific examples of well-written humor, he shows his readers how they, too, can make their readers laugh out loud.
> **Dena Dyer**, speaker and author whose work has appeared in such magazines as *Women's World, Nick Jr., Writer's Digest*

www.denadyer.com

Laugh and learn your way through *Writing With Banana Peels*! I recommend it.

Anita Higman, author of *Love Finds You in Humble Texas*
www.anitahigman.com

Funny, funny stuff, but also packed with practical lessons and insight. Jim openly shares comedy secrets used to achieve success in speaking, satire, and assorted silliness.

Torry Martin
Actor, comic, writer for *Adventures in Odyssey*
www.torrymartin.com

This is not a [book] to be tossed aside lightly. It should be thrown with great force.

Dorothy Parker (1893-1967), book reviewer for *Esquire*

A milk-out-the-nose funny book for both writers *and* readers.

Rhonda Rhea, author of *The Purse-uit of Holiness*, *High Heels on High Places*, and *Amusing Grace.*
www.rhondarhea.org

James Watkins, nationally-known writing coach, author, and speaker unpeels the methods behind the madness of writing humor writing with inspiration, tips, and side-splitting anecdotes.

Ronna Snyder, speaker and award-winning author of *Hot Flashes from Heaven*
www.ronnasnyder.com

Jim is an author, speaker, and self-described "threat to society." What makes him so dangerous is his felonious faith and sinister sense of humor.

Al Speegle, columnist for *The Wittenburg Door: the World's Pretty Much Only Religious Satire Magazine*
(www.wittenburgdoor.com) alspeegle.wordpress.com

Writing with Banana Peels: Principles, Practices, and Pratfalls of Writing Humor

James N. Watkins

XarisCom

Dedication

To my dad, Donald James Watkins,
who gave me the gene for dry English humor.
What a gift! Thanks!

Contents

Foreword

This is my very first time to write a foreword for a book, but there's a first time for everything. Sort of like the first time this Alaskan hippie turned Christian comedian made jewelry from moose droppings and discovered there's a huge market of gullible tourists looking for truly tacky souvenirs.

And, now that I think of it, there are many remarkable similarities between making moose dropping jewelry and comedy writing. They are both an art form that takes effort and imagination. Both also involve getting your hands dirty by handling things that others would never touch. You also need the ability to look at something from a completely different angle. And just like moose droppings, some jokes are hard to find while others you simply step right into. Some stink and crumble easily while others will stand the test of time. And others, no matter how much love and effort you put into polishing them, they will never be appreciated by everyone.

Writing with Bananas, however, is amazing. Funny, funny stuff, but also packed with practical lessons and insight. Jim openly shares comedy secrets used to achieve success in speaking, satire, and assorted silliness. His unique style of writing teaches and delights at the same time. Somehow his instructional methods feel less like a class and more like a conversation over a cup of coffee with a thoughtful friend.

Midway through the book, I found myself wishing it had been printed several years ago. Everything I learned about comedy I learned through books while I was living in a remote cabin in Alaska. If Jim's book had been in print back then you could have saved me a lot of money on Amazon! And I could have started on the comedy circuit—and given up my moose dropping jewelry career—much earlier.

Torry Martin
Actor, comic, writer for *Adventures in Odyssey*
www.torrymartin.com

Introduction

*Humor can be dissected, as a frog can,
but the thing dies in the process and the innards are
discouraging to any but the pure scientific mind.*
E B White

I have in my right hand, direct from my home office in Corn Borer, Indiana, the top ten reasons to read this book:

10. You'll read a bunch of funny stuff from Dave Barry, Martha Bolton, Stephen Colbert, Bill Cosby, Torry Martin, Rhonda Rhea, Will Rogers, Steven Wright, and many more.

9. People will like you more when you write with humor.

8. You'll be healthier and so will your readers.

7. Your writing will be 10 percent more memorable with humor.

6. You'll learn how to drill away on touchy subjects by using laughing gas.

5. You can impress your snooty academic friends who think humor writers are intellectual light weights by quoting Plato, Aristotle, Schopenhauer, and Freud on their philosophies of humor.

4. You'll learn how to connect with and comfort your readers.

3. You'll be encouraged that nothing terrible happens to authors—just terrific anecdotes. (Nothing says comedy like a kidney stone!)

2. You'll become rich and famous, lose weight, whiten your teeth, stop global warming, save the whales, realize world peace, and learn the comic technique of hyperbole.

1. You'll earn back the price of this book with your humor writing or your money back.

This book is the result of teaching dangerously-creative college students at Taylor University. That's surprising in that a) writing humor is actually offered for college credit, b) parents will actually pay their hard-earned money for Junior to take such a class, and—most amazing—c) the study of humor is considered a scholarly pursuit worthy of federal funding!

It has been so much fun and hopefully an educational experience that will better prepare my students for an exciting career at Starbucks.

And you, too, can learn to make minimum wage writing humor. And I guarantee—or your money back—you will be 100 percent satisfied as you receive emails like this:

> WOW! We LOVE your relevant and insightful take on what is going on in the world around us along with the witty presentation (tongue and cheek humor) that you use to drive a point home. We often have been in stitches at your puns. We've passed along your articles to others that may benefit from your humor. Keep up the good work and keep the endorphins flowing!
> csx24him@aol.com

I just read your "Church Bailouts Circa 2019." What a hoot. I'm having a difficult time containing the laughter to ease the face pain. I loved it. I would love to share it with my friends and would of course give you full credit and include a link to your website.

ronfurg@cox.net

Tony and I laughed till we had tears going down our faces when you referred to 2008 as "The Year of the Shop Vac: It sucked!" So glad you were able to find some humor in such a situation, but God pulls us through!

mooey01@hotmail.com

So, that's my purpose in writing this book: to help you, too, bring pain and tears to your readers. And along the way entertainment and encouragement!

Enjoy!

1
Serious studies of humor: Plato to Freud to . . .

Humor is the only test of gravity, and gravity of humor;
for a subject which will not bear raillery is suspicious,
and a jest which will not bear serious examination is false wit.
Aristotle

Your hard-earned tax dollars are actually funding university professors to engage in serious studies of humor. I know, I know, "serious studies of humor" sounds like an oxymoron such as jumbo shrimp, airline food, and government intelligence.

Here are just a few of the offerings at major universities:

"Humor and Laughter" at Arkansas State University

"The Rhetoric of American Political Humor" at the University of Maryland

"Communication and Humor" at Concordia College

"The Psychology of Humour and Laughter" at Queens University in Belfast

"The Arts and Science of Humor" at Truman University

"Enhance Your Teaching with Laughter" University of California at Santa Cruz

"Humor: An Interdisciplinary Approach" at Holy Names College

And, of course, "Writing Humor" at Taylor University in beautiful downtown Upland, Indiana.

There's also an academic conference sponsored by The International Society for Humor Studies with its journal: *Humor:*

International Journal of Humor Research with juried papers on:

"Disparagement Humor: A Theoretical and Empirical Review of Psychoanalytic, Superiority, and Social Identity Theories"

"The Fear of Being Laughed at: Individual and Group Differences in Gelotophobia"

"Humor, Emotional Intelligence, Social Competence, and Psychological Well-Being"

And, if you don't have plans in June, you can attend the conference at California State University at Long Beach.

So, for all your snooty friends who think humor is all about knock-knock jokes, whoopee cushions, and plastic doggie doo doo, let them know that . . .

Humor is serious business

The first records we have of humor as an academic discipline are the writings of Aristotle around 500 BC.

Humor is the only test of gravity, and gravity of humor; for a subject which will not bear raillery is suspicious, and a jest which will not bear serious examination is false wit.

Like most of Aristotle's writing, you'll need to read that twice, but humor has been taken seriously for at least twenty-five hundred years. During that time, other philosophers have studied humor and developed over one hundred theories of why humor is, well, humorous.

Neurosurgeons have also gotten involved in humor research. Dr. Walter van den Broek, a Dutch psychiatrist, claims that humor is a five-stage process in our brains:

1. The stimulus contains the potential elements of humor
2. Stimulus is perceived as humorous
3. Stimulus leads to exhilaration
4. The motor expression of laughter is prompted
5. And elevated mood is produced.

The good doctor goes on to locate the specific areas of the brain involved since this a "complicated process" with each of the five elements having their own "cerebral substrate."

The frontal and temporal regions are involved in the perception of humor. These, in turn, would induce facial reactions and laughter mediated by dorsal brainstem regions. These reactions would be inhibited by the ventral brainstem, probably via frontal motor/premotor areas.

[An] MRI study has found mesolimbic reward activation associated with humorous cartoons, providing a neurobiological link between theories of humor and hedonic processes in the brain.

I have no idea what that means, but it makes me feel so much smarter, as a humor writer, just to type it!

Four early theories of humor
1. **Incongruity** was addressed in Aristotle's classic work, *Rhetoric.* In it he taught that the best way to get an audience to laugh is to set up an expectation and deliver something "that gives a twist."
In his book, *Judgment,* German philosopher Immanuel Kant (1724-1804) writes about humor being derived from incongruity:

In everything that is to excite a lively laugh there must be something absurd (in which the understanding, therefore, can find no satisfaction). Laughter is an affection arising from the sudden transformation of a strained expectation into nothing.

Finally, another German philosopher, Arthur Schopenhauer (1788–1860), wrote that humor resulted from surprise: "The sudden perception of incongruity." (See, I told you humor is serious business!)

Here's an example of using incongruity for comic results that I've had published in several magazines and have posted on YouTube.com:

We're Pro-Choice

This past election season we heard a lot about the importance of everyone having the "right to choose." We, too, want to avoid "legislating values" and forcing "moral absolutes" upon our good citizens.

Ethics is a personal choice, not a political or religious concern. That's why we've established "Planned Bank Robbery." Now, we personally don't approve of bank robbery, but we don't want to inflict our morals on anyone else either.

It must be a personal decision of each individual.

Education is the key since our studies reveal that 99 percent of senior high teens know that banks are robbed. But it is shocking the number of teens who don't know *how* banks are robbed. Or even how to load a .357 magnum, drive a get-away car, or demand, "Give me all of your unmarked, non-sequentially-ordered twenty-dollar bills." Young people need to know the wide range of career options available to them.

And we're also concerned that a lot of young people are robbing banks without proper protection. Personal injury and irresponsibility are much greater crimes than actually knocking over the First National. At Planned Bank Robbery we don't approve of unauthorized withdrawals. But we do want to offer—free of charge—bullet-proof vests, ski masks, and if necessary a reliable get-away car. This is the compassionate thing to do!

And young people who need some extra cash from their local 7-Eleven shouldn't have to get their parent's permission to obtain this protection. If that were the case, hundreds more teens would be needlessly injured by narrow-minded parents who are trying to inflict their morality on their children.

Again, let me emphasize that Planned Bank Robbery does not condone or encourage grand larceny. We only want to stress it is a personal decision. We're "pro-choice"!

Copyright © 1986 James N. Watkins

When you take the "pro-choice" argument and apply to virtually any other issue, it makes absolutely no sense.

Here's another example, also in print at jameswatkins.com and on YouTube.com:

Yep! I'm Intolerant

Hi. I'm Jim. I'm coming out of the politically correct closet and announcing to the world, "Yep, I'm intolerant!"

For instance, do you really want to go to an "open-minded" doctor with signs in the waiting room that read: "I Brake for Bacteria," "Save the Salmonella," or "Take a Stand for Polio"?! I want a doctor who is narrow-minded and completely intolerant to disease and physical afflictions when I'm told, "Turn your head and cough."

And I'm not getting on a plane with a pilot who comes over the intercom with, "Welcome aboard Lame Duck Airlines. We'll be traveling at whatever speed and altitude feels good at the time and should be arriving at our destina . . . destina . . . airport bar in time for "happy hour." So, put your seat in recline position, hold on tight to your carry-ons, and we'll be ready for take-off as soon as we cut off that 747 on our way to the runaway." (Where did he say the emergency exits were?!)

How about a tolerant mechanic at the brake shop?

"I don't like to use the words 'safe' or 'unsafe' when it comes to brake shoes. I prefer to think of them having mechanical diversity."

Or a tolerant math teacher?

"Well, Johnny if 2 + 2 is 5 for you, then I'm not going to put any moral judgments on your mathematical world view."

I don't even want to think about tolerant parachute packers, nuclear power plant operators, or driver's ed. teachers ("Stop signs are arbitrary restrictions on our personal freedom.")

Most of all, I'm down right intolerant when it comes to my kids. If I really love them, I'm going to be narrow-minded toward anything that is harmful to their physical, mental, social, and spiritual well-being. That's why I'm judgmental toward plaque build up, kiddy porn, gangs, strep throat, "put-downs," under-cooked hamburgers, spaced-out cults, illegal drugs, and nicotine (tobacco execs are simply serial killers in suits).

You're welcomed to be tolerant of this column. You can tape it to your refrigerator or use it to housebreak your new puppy. Somehow civilization will manage to continue despite your judgment of my writing.

But I'm not so sure that our society will continue if "Thou shalt not be intolerant" becomes the eleventh commandment. Perhaps we could be a bit more narrow-minded in observing the first ten.

Copyright © 1997 James N. Watkins

2. **Superiority** was a second theory of humor championed by Plato (circa 428 BC to 347 BC) who was Aristotle's mentor. He writes in *Philebus* that the "mixture of pleasure and pain that lies in the *malice* of amusement"—the "Junior-High" school of humor.

In *Rhetoric,* Aristotle defines wit as "educated insolence." (I reference these works just to assure you—and the dean—that I've done careful research on this scholarly silliness). In *Nicomachean Ethics,* he describes jokes as "a kind of abuse" that should ideally be told without producing pain.

English philosopher Thomas Hobbes (1588-1679) is best known for providing the basis of Western political philosophy with his "social contract" theory. But in *Human Nature* he wrote:

> The passion of laughter is nothing else but sudden glory arising from some sudden conception of some eminency in ourselves, by comparison with the infirmity of others, or with our own formerly.

Sigmund Freud (1856-1939)—the pioneer in psychoanalysis and phallic symbols—also pontificated on the "superiority" theory of humor.

> A good bit of humor is oriented to maintaining the status quo by ridiculing deviant social behavior and reassuring the majority that their way of life is proper. It is used as a weapon of the "ins" against the "outs."

Again, the teasing, being made fun of, and social ridicule of junior high!

Robert Solomon, a philosophy professor at Princeton and recently at the University of Texas at Austin, argued against the "superiority theory" with his "inferiority theory." He believed our recognition of our silly antics and self-deprecation is based on inferiority or modesty. He points out there is nothing superior about "The Three Stooges." (I would argue that we laugh at Larry, Moe and Curly because we feel *superior* to their collective IQ of a zucchini. Which takes us right back to the superiority theory.)

As someone who tries to apply the Golden Rule to life—and humor—I'm not providing any examples of superiority humor. You can find plenty on television, online, and in print.

3. **Relief theory** is based on premise that humor is a psychological process. Freud believed—apart from making us feel superior—all laughter results from a release of excessive energy or tension. In "Jokes and Their Relation to the

Unconscious," he—of course—managed to work sex into his theory: "The energy that would have been used to repress sexual and hostile feelings is saved and can be released in laughter."

In *The Physiology of Laughter,* English philosopher Herbert Spencer (1820-1903) described this as the "hydraulic" theory of nervous energy is which excitement and mental agitation produces energy that "must expend itself in some way or another."

We see this in "comic relief" in Indiana Jones or other high-suspense films. In Zambia, where I was reporting on the HIV/AIDS crisis, we were warned that people laugh at tragic situations. They seem to love sketches. So, when in a sketch a husband left his wife after *he* infected her with HIV/AIDS—which is all too common—the audience exploded in laughter! And not nervous titters, but full-blown belly laughter.

The strongest arguments against the relief theory is that a) most humor is sudden, without a build up of energy, 2) sustained laughter—an hour and a half romantic comedy or standup act—wouldn't produce laughter after the first release of energy, and 3) Freud was a sexually-obsessed neurotic.

That said, I tend to subscribe to the release theory. When I was diagnosed with cancer in 2008, I immediately began looking for some humor to mine.

Lessons from Lower-Case c

It's been nearly six months since my doctor sat Lois and me down in his office, somberly looked through his manila folder, and announced, "Well, the bad news is you have cancer. The good news is that we caught it as early as possible and it's completely treatable and not life-threatening."

So, I have in my right hand, direct from my home office in Corn Borer, Indiana, **top ten things I've learned living with cancer**:

10. Cancer is a great way to get out of work!

"Sorry, I can't help with VBS. I'm having radiation for prostate cancer." One editor actually offered to delay a deadline if I didn't feel up to writing. And Lois mowed the lawn several times this summer. Nobody is going to argue with you when you beg out with "I've got cancer."

9. I get my very own month—and exclusive club

Yah, yah, October is Breast Cancer Month with all the pink ribbons and major media coverage, but did you know that September is Prostate Cancer Month? Don't feel badly—it's a well-kept secret. Probably because men are not about to wear little blue ribbons announcing to the world there's trouble in Mansylvania!

But you also become part of an exclusive club—no girls allowed! Sort of like those old veterans who have an instant camaraderie at the VFW post. I've been amazed at the number of men who've come forward to share that they too have fought the battle of prostate cancer.

8. I still haven't mastered waiting

To me, hell would be sitting in a waiting room for eternity.

A year of waiting for multiple PSA results, all a bit higher than the last. Waiting for a biopsy. Waiting for the biopsy results. Waiting for treatment to begin once the doctor dropped the C-bomb. Waiting for the final results. I had my last "zap" August 28 and will finally get results—after a two-month wait—tomorrow.

And then waiting one to two years to see if the nuclear attack on Mansylvania will affect Watertown and Loveland.

I'll post the results of the treatment as soon as I know them, so thanks for waiting with me and especially your prayers. I don't do waiting well, but I have felt a miraculous peace during this time. And for that, I am grateful—and amazed.

7. Cancer comes with a capital C and with a lower case c

Prostate cancer is the lazy, under-achiever in the cancer family: it lives in the basement of its parent's home; slow-growing and easily defeated if caught early. You don't even "battle" it at my stage. You simply lie back and let the radioactive waves zap the little slacker. It's cancer with a lower-case c.

So, my heart goes out to those who are facing Cancer with a capital, underlined C: those in terrible pain as they wage a life-and-death battle with the monster, who have been told they have six months to live and who will never see their children or grandchildren grow up. I've probably been too flippant about my diagnosis and treatment in my blog posts. Sorry!

6. It may be lower case, but it's still a life-changer

We all need a "wake up call" that life is short and unpredictable, that God and family are the most important things in life, and that we need to leave the world a better place than we found it.

I'm grateful mine has been a tap on the shoulder, not a blow to the gut that leaves one breathless, immobilized and dying. (And there *is* a 5 percent chance the radiation treatment will not have been effective and I will have less than ten years left on this earth—I did mention it is a *slow* cancer.)

And so I will try to write faster, love my God and family deeper, and live more fully after my wake up call. And I pray your wake up call will be in all lower-case letters!

5. I can now relate to more people than ever

I love 2 Corinthians 1:3-4:

Praise be to the God and Father of our Lord
Jesus Christ, the Father of compassion and the God
of all comfort, who comforts us in all our troubles,
so that we can comfort those in any trouble with
the comfort we ourselves have received from God.

I can now relate to those with chronic fatigue. For a
few weeks I was completely worn out and took more naps
than our chow-shep-sky. (As the cancer cells die, toxins
are released into the blood stream, creating fatigue, so the
worse you feel, the better.) I now know what it feels like
to be completely depleted with not one once of strength in
reserve.

I can now relate to all those people on the commercials
during the evening news with "painful, frequent urges."
The fatigue can be greatly reduced by drinking gallons of
water—which, of course, creates its own side-effect. But I
was able to keep up with my writing and editing deadlines
between trips to the bathroom—for which I'm thankful. (It
helps that my home office is right across from the
bathroom.)

And, I can now relate to those with mental handicaps.
My family dubbed it "radiation retardation." The physical
stress of being bombarded with 60 rads of radiation every
day, created real mental stress. I got to the point where I
couldn't add up a simple column of numbers. It was
frightening, frustrating, humiliating and depressing. I *think*
I'm over it, but I'll let you be the judge.

So, I'm now able to comfort those with the comfort
I've received from God, family, and friends.

4. I'm grateful for "little" miracles

I have sensed so many little ways God has worked
through all this. The cancer was caught as early as
possible and is one of the most successfully treated kinds
of cancer. God cleared my summer speaking schedule.

The kabillion-dollar, high-tech, laser-guided, computer-programmed radiation machine is just four minutes from our house. In the summer, there are no issues with snow and ice in the early morning. The staff at Progressive Cancer Care was indeed "caring," compassionate, and had a great sense of humor. And, I have a home office just four seconds from the bathroom. So, for all of these blessings, I'm extremely thankful!

3. **God doesn't answer everyone's prayers**

My friend, Dennis, died of a brain tumor, even though hundreds of people prayed—and some even fasted—for him, the elders anointed him with oil, and he had faith much larger than a mustard seed. And he still died.

In fact, while Lois and I were pastoring a small church in northern Indiana, ten wonderful, godly people got cancer and everyone of them died—in spite of prayer, fasting, anointing, and faith.

So, I don't have a money-back, 100-percent-satisfaction guarantee of good news tomorrow. The only thing I'm promised is that . . .

2. **God is in control**

So, as I write this the night before my PSA test, one part of me is holding on to the doctors' prognosis that radiation treatment is 95 percent successful. Another part of me is thinking, "There are those five poor stiffs who won't have successful results." (And everyone I talk to who has had radiation treatment have had wonderful results. So where are the 5 percent?!)

Whatever the answer is tomorrow, God is in control. I don't know how many times I've played the Twila Paris song, "God is in control. We believe that His children will not be forsaken. God is in control. We will choose to remember, and never be shaken."

Yes, God is in control and Romans 8:28-29 is still

in effect:

"And we know that in all things God works for the good of those who love him, who have been called according to his purpose . . . to be conformed to the likeness of his Son."

1. **I've realized how many friends I have**

I love the scene from *It's a Wonderful Life* where the word goes out that "George Bailey is in trouble." The entire town gathers to pray and pour out their love.

I've been completely overwhelmed with the emails and cards expressing love and promising that I am being prayed for daily. And even several envelopes with large checks to help with medical expenses. (The very day I started radiation treatments, Lois had an emergency hysterectomy.)

It is a wonderful life when you have the love of God, family, and friends. Thank you for walking with me on this journey.

Tomorrow . . . the results! 3 PM Eastern; 2 PM Central.

Okay, it not milk-out-your-nose funny, but at least it was good therapy. And, I thank my heavenly Father that I'm cancer free.

4. **Play theory** was championed by Max Eastman. He was an anti-establishment, socialist poet, who decided after living in Russia for a year, Communism wasn't all the comrades claimed it was, and became an advocate for the free-enterprise system

In, *The Enjoyment of Laughter*, he argued that "we come into the world endowed with an instinctive tendency to laugh and have this feeling in response to pains presented playfully."

According to his theory, humor requires taking a disinterested attitude towards what might otherwise be seen as serious. Humor is the playground of the mind

Modern theories

Humor scholars—another great oxymoron—have not been content with just four theories (incongruity, superiority, release and play), so have created over one hundred theories.

The most recent is Patricia Keith-Spiegel's classification of humor theories into eight major types:

1. **Biological** humor is *not* junior-high potty humor involving boogers and body parts. Keith-Spiegel argues laughter is hard-wired into our bodies. It's a function of the nervous system to stimulate, relax, and restore a sense of well-being; a first-cousin to the "Release" theory

2. **Superiority** (Yep, covered that.)

3. **Incongruity** (Covered that, too.)

4. **Surprise** would be playing "Peek-a-boo" with a two-year-old or the surreptitious placing of a whoopee cushion by a *twenty*-two-year old.

Max Eastman wrote:

> A joke is not a thing but a process, a trick you play on the listener's mind. You start him off toward a plausible goal, and then by a sudden twist you land him nowhere at all or just where he didn't expect to go.

5. **Ambivalence** is "the result of opposing emotions or ideas within an appreciator." Incongruity is the conflict of ideas or perceptions, while ambivalence is the conflict of emotions: love/hate relationships.

6. **Release** was also covered earlier.

7. **Configuration** is the opposite of number 3 in that the humor derives from the *resolution of* incongruities. Max Eastman explains, "Laughter is, after speech, the chief thing that holds society together."

8. **Psychoanalytic**

Differs slightly from number 6, in that laughter results from *repressed* psychic energy. Perhaps that's why we laugh at sexual or obscene humor.

So there you have the scholarly study of humor. I feel so much smarter after writing it and I hope you feel so much smarter after reading it!

2

The medical, educational, and psycho-social benefits of humor

A cheerful heart is good medicine,
but a crushed spirit dries up the bones.
Proverbs 17:22

I always wonder the reaction of parents when they discover their hard-earned money is paying for Junior to take a class called "Eng 460 Writing Humor." Maybe you're wondering, *What was I thinking when I bought a book called* Writing with Banana Peels*?!*

Never fear! Humor is actually beneficial on several fronts:

Humor improves your health

Voltaire, a French writer and philosopher from the 1700s, noted: "The art of medicine consists of keeping the patient amused while nature heals the disease." (I keep quoting long-dead scholars and philosophers to convince myself that writing humor is a *serious* and completely *respectable* endeavor.)

More recently, Dr. Paul E. McGhee, in his book *Health, Healing and the Amuse System,* documents the health benefits of humor:

Humor strengthens the immune system. Laughter increases immunoglobulin A, a part of your immune system which protects you against upper respiratory problems, like colds and the flu. Humor also increases T-cells which seek out and destroy tumor cells, viruses, and foreign organisms.

Humor reduces food cravings. (I'll have to do more study on that as soon as I finish my daily dosage of dark chocolate.)

Humor reduces pain and increases one's threshold for pain. Norman Cousins' book, *Anatomy of an Illness*, documents how a spinal disease left him in almost constant pain. He discovered that moving out of a dreary hospital and into a cheery hotel room, where he watched "Candid Camera" and comedy films, eased his pain. He specifically denied that humor "cured" anything and repeatedly reminded his readers that he took all the medications, along with high doses of vitamin C, prescribed by his doctors.

But he did claim in his last book, *Head First: the Biology of Hope,* that ten minutes of belly laughter gave him two hours of pain-free sleep.

Over a dozen studies have now documented that humor does have the power to reduce pain in many patients. One study surveyed thirty-five patients in a rehabilitation hospital suffering from such conditions as traumatic brain injury, spinal cord injury, arthritis, limb amputations, and a range of other neurological or musculoskeletal disorders. Nearly three-fourths (74 percent) agreed with the statement, "Sometimes laughing works as well as a pain pill."

The most commonly given explanation is that laughter causes the production of endorphins, one of the body's natural pain killers. However, medical kill-joys point out that only two scientific studies have been conducted on this claim, and each failed to show any increase in endorphins.

In June 2008, Basil Hugh Hall addressed this in his paper "Laughter as a displacement activity: the implications for humor theory." While he states that laughter does *not* produce endorphins, he writes, "Recent advances in imaging techniques have enabled researchers to demonstrate an increase in opioids in the brain after strenuous exercise (Boecker et al 2008), and there is no reason to dismiss the idea that a similar increase in the brain's opioids will be found after a laughter evoking event." (So, please, while reading this book, don't submit to a drug test!)

Humor reduces level of stress hormones such as cortisol, epinephrine (adrenaline), dopamine, and growth hormone.

Humor is a cardio-vascular workout. Some have called laughter "internal jogging" which may reduce blood pressure. There's even an emerging therapeutic field known as "humor therapy."

(Dr. Steven M. Sultanoff has an excellent Web site documenting humor's therapeutic effects at: www.humormatters.com/articles.htm.)

Humor improves communication

This is why I'm glad Taylor has included "Writing Humor" in its professional writing program. Humor improves communication in all disciplines.

I actually wrote a paper in graduate school called, "Effectiveness of the Use of Humor on Persuasive Messages in Print." It cited university studies claiming that. . .

Humor attracts attention in all types of persuasive messages: advertising, politics, debating with your seventeen-year-old daughter.

Humor increases likeability of the source, but doesn't necessarily enhance source credibility. (People love clowns, but don't elect them to office. Okay, bad example.)

Humor doubles the persuasiveness of a message. According to a 1990 study by Biel and Brigwater, individuals who liked an advertisement were twice as likely to be persuaded to act upon it.

Humor increases comprehension in education. In 1990, Gortham and Christophel set up an experiment in "Introduction to Statistics" classes. (Now there's a coma-inducing subject!) Two classes were taught by the same professor using the same text and syllabus, but in one class relevant humor was used and the other class included no humor.

I'm not exactly sure what "statistical humor" involves.

"Two binary variables walk into a bar. . . ."

"What did the hetereoscedastic data say to the homoscedastic data?"

"How many dummy variables does it take to screw in a light bulb?"

But I digress. Researchers found that in the class using humor, students scored 10 percent higher than their counterparts!

Humor causes listeners/readers to lower their defenses. Think of humor as "laughing gas" that allows you to drill away at sensitive subjects as we'll see later.

Humor makes you smarter

James Lyttle also claims:

> The creation and appreciation of humor has long been associated with high intelligence, problem solving, creativity, generativity, and high verbal ability. Humor involves the suspension of the normal rules of logic, as does innovation and has been shown to enhance mental rotation.

I have no idea what "mental rotation" is, but I suddenly feel so much better about being a humor writer. You and I are highly intelligent people who surpass the normal rules of logic! (And you thought you were just the class clown!)

However, I think I just pulled a hemisphere just writing about the psychological and neurological aspects of humor. (If you want to explore more, visit Dr. Lyttle's fascinating site www.jimlyttle.com/Humor.html and www.humorlinks.com. Mind stretching stuff!)

Humor connects with readers

Using humor, then, literally creates good feelings in our readers and listeners. Equally powerful in humor, is the awareness of, "I've felt that same way" or "That happens to my family all the time." The best sitcoms and standup routines are funny because we see ourselves—or more often others—in the humorous situation.

It brings a sense of connection. We have something in common, even if it only is our eccentric uncles.

Humor comforts our readers

Best-selling humorist Barbara Johnson is a prime example of the concept "comedy is tragedy plus time." Someday we're going to laugh about it! Barbara has experienced more pain and loss than most spouses or parents, and yet she is able to write with wit and warmth that comforts her readers.

Erma Bombeck would agree. "Laughter rises out of tragedy, when you need it the most, and rewards you for your courage."

And David Meuer writes:

I believe that when I make someone laugh, I give them a gift. Because sometimes life can be hard and scary and depressing. People really need to have laughter in their lives—and they especially need to laugh about the very things that can make us want to rip out our hair by the handfuls. Our kids. That thing our spouse does that bugs us. Our church family. Our job. Our lemon of a station wagon.

So, our shared experience, told in a witty rather than whining manner, comforts. The apostle Paul writes:

We can comfort those in any trouble with the comfort we ourselves have received from God (2 Corinthians 1:1-4).

Here's a column that came out of extreme pain, but continues to comfort readers:

Everyone needs a kidney stone

Everyone needs to have a kidney stone once in his or her life time; preferably, the sooner the better.

You see, experiencing the sensation of having a semi tractor-trailer with snow chains and a load of rolled steel

park on your lower back tends to put life into perspective.

For instance, if you're riding in a tour bus and the rest room door suddenly swings open, and you can't reach the handle without creating an additional sight on the tour, you can say, "Hey, sure beats a kidney stone." (All of these examples are, of course, hypothetical and have never happened to me personally.) Or your daughter calls you at 1 AM in the middle of winter and says, "Uh, Dad, did you know that a '95 Neon can straddle a traffic island?" you can say, "Hey, sure beats a kidney stone."

This perspective also works for times you attempt to repair the toilet yourself and manage to not only cripple the commode, but break off the main water shut-off valve. (I did mention that these are strictly hypothetical examples, didn't I?)

It helps when your mother-in-law backs into your brand-new car. The time your five-year-old son drives spikes into your coffee table. When you lose a great job as an editor at a publishing house due to corporate down-sizing. While you're recovering from double-hernia surgery and something on TV prompts a belly laugh. When you're spending half your vacation time sitting in a traffic jam in downtown Chicago with a stick shift, no air-conditioning, and two kids in the back seat waging a fight to the death. You can always say, "Hey, sure beats a kidney stone."

It also works for intestinal flu, crashed computers, lactose intolerance, sadistic dental hygienists, arthritis, overdrawn checking accounts, terminal toasters and transmissions, impacted wisdom teeth extractions, IRS audits, and flat tires in the rain fifty miles from any form of civilization.

Now there are some things that are worse than a

kidney stone such as death, divorce, and "Saved by the Bell" reruns, but most domestic disasters and occupational pratfalls pale in comparison to a kidney stone. And that puts everything in perfect perspective.

It's been six years since my painful epiphany, which brings me to another kidney stone insight: "All things must pass."

Copyright © 1997 James N. Watkins

Humor confronts our readers

I wrote earlier that German philosopher Arthur Schopenhaur claimed that laughter is the "sudden perception of incongruity" between our ideals and our behavior.

When I was attending Ball State graduate classes, one of the students kept arguing "Well, you know, there are no absolutes." I finally got so tired of that argument, that I wrote this column:

Are you absolutely sure there are no absolutes?

A while ago, David Samuels wrote in the *New York Times* magazine—and I quote—"It is a shared if unspoken premise of the world that most of us inhabit that absolutes do not exist and that people who claim to have found them are crazy."

Being the "crazy" person that I am, I honestly don't understand the following tenants of the truly tolerant like Mr. Samuels.

"There is no such thing as absolute truth."

Help me understand this. You're saying it's absolutely true that there's no absolute truth. And if that's true, how can you be sure your statement is truth?

"I only believe what I can perceive with my five senses."

Hmmm? Can you prove that statement by sight, smell, hearing, touch, or taste? I don't think so.

"What is right and wrong are for the individual to decide."

Okay, so rapper R. Kelly, who allegedly had child pornography on his computer, shouldn't be harassed by intolerant authorities because pictures of naked 12-year-olds are "right" for him? And that wacky Iraqi, Saddam Hussein, is simply expressing his individuality by using chemical weapons on his own people and taking his sons out for a night of torturing political prisoners.

Aren't there some things that are always wrong for everyone? And if you say "yes," aren't you admitting to a "moral absolute"? If you say "no," I'm assuming it's okay with you if I steal your wallet.

"Well, right and wrong is what a society decides it is."

Hmmm? So slavery was right for thousands of years until society recently decided it wasn't? How about segregation? Was that just fine until a majority in Congress decided it wasn't in 1964? And why are we hassling societies of China, North Korea, and Sudan for the torture and murder of religious minorities?

"No, something is wrong if it hurts other people."

Wait a minute. I thought you said there were no moral absolutes? Is that always true for all cultures? Aren't suicide bombers in the Middle East idolized as moral heroes by a part of society?

And how 'bout the person in a mask who comes up to you, knocks you unconscious, slashes open your chest, and takes all your money? Of course I'm talking about a cardiologist. So, isn't some pain good for us? Isn't "hurt" an absolute concept? And what about sado-masochism?

"Well, you shouldn't try to change other people's beliefs."

But what if I disagree with that statement? Aren't you trying to change my beliefs?

Let me get this straight, it's "right" for you to try to

convince me of your ideas about "no absolute truth" and "individual morality," but it's "wrong" for me to try to take my beliefs out into the arena of public debate?

"You're just intolerant!"

So, you're saying I'm intolerant for simply voicing my beliefs, but you're "tolerant" for rejecting my views as "intolerant"?

Hmmm? Are you absolutely sure about that?!

So tell your parents or spouse, that by taking this class and buying this book, you'll actually be healthier and cut medical expenses, be a more persuasive person, a better teacher, a more compassionate person . . .

3

Is there such a thing as 'Christian' humor?

I am all in favor of laughing. Laughing has something in it in common with the ancient words of faith and inspiration; it unfreezes pride and unwinds secrecy; it makes men forget themselves in the presence of something greater than themselves.
G. K. Chesterton

Every syllabus at Taylor University must include a statement on "Integration of Faith and Learning." So, what's the "Christian" basis for using humor?

Well, Proverbs 17:22 teaches, "A cheerful heart is good medicine," while Job 8:21 promises, "He will yet fill your mouth with laughter."

But the strongest argument of all is this: Jesus was a standup comic. Really!

The hip humor in first century Palestine was hyperbole or intentional exaggeration. So when Jesus talked about people who ". . . strain out a gnat but swallow a camel" or look for speck in someone's eye, when they have a *log* in his or her eye, He had them rolling on the hillsides!

And ridiculous situations are always good for a laugh: pulling a camel through the eye of a needle, hiding a lamp (an open flame) under a bed (a dry grass mat), etc.

Elton Trueblood, the author of the fascinating book *The Humor of Christ,* notes that Jesus' parable of the "Shrewd

Steward" (Luke 16) is either completely contradictory to the rest of scripture—Jesus seems to tell his disciples to be dishonest and use money to bribe and make friends—or He is being satirical. He writes in *The Yoke of Christ*:

So long as we think Jesus was always serious, there is no reasonable way of making sense out of the advice to make friends with unrighteous mammon, but, if we recognize satire, the whole matter is clear. Probably the disciples laughed as they listened. In a modern paraphrase His satirical passage would be easily understandable. "You want to get ahead, do you? Then do it thoroughly. If you make bribes, make big ones and cover your tracks. Always use cash and never a check. If you are going to steal, don't steal from a bank. Steal the bank itself and then you may receive a doctor's degree!" However modern this seems, it is as old as human history and it is precisely what Christ's sharp satire implies. Perhaps he found it took satire to make the disciples see the point.

Effective Christian communicators such as G. K. Chesterton have often used humor. When someone scolded Charles Spurgeon for using humor in his sermons, the late, great preacher answered, "This preacher think it less of a crime to cause a momentary laughter than a half hour of profound slumber."

But what makes Christian humor, well, Christian. Here's a great answer from Madeline L'Engle recorded in *Walking on Water*. When asked, "What makes Christian writing Christian?" she answered:

I told her that if she is truly and deeply a Christian, what she writes in going to be Christian, whether she mentions Jesus or not. And if she is not, in the most profound sense, Christian, then what she writes is not going to be Christian, no matter how many times she invokes the name of the Lord.

The apostle Paul also gives us some insight in Colossians 4:5-6:

> Be wise in the way you act toward outsiders; make the most of every opportunity. Let your conversation be always full of grace, seasoned with salt, so that you may know how to answer everyone.

I try to ask myself—when writing for either Christian or secular market—"Will this draw the reader closer to Jesus or push them farther away?" So, when I was writing a book on the after-life called *Death & Beyond,* I was tempted to call the chapter on actress Shirley MacLain's reincarnation book, *Out on a Limb,* "Out of Her Tree." But what, if by the providence of God, she picks up the book. Would my "conversation" draw her closer to Jesus or push her farther away?

And Jesus is described by John as "full of truth and *grace.*" Paul writes about only "speaking the truth in *love.*"

Maybe I'm finally getting the hang of the balancing act of truth and grace. I have a column on my Web site called "God hates godhatesfags.com." It's a rebuttal of Fred Phelps' "God hates fags" picketing at public events—including military funerals.

I had a young man email to thank me for the post:

"First, I want you to know that I'm a gay agnostic. But if there is a God, I want Him to be the kind of God you describe."

So, are there certain subjects "off limits" to Christian authors? I don't think so. For instance, after I had signed the contract for *Death & Beyond* and cashed—and spent—the generous advance, an editor at Tyndale House called to say, "Oh, I forgot to mention, be sure to include lots of humor so it doesn't get too depressing."

"I'm sorry. I must have a bad connection. I thought you said you want a book for students on death to include lots of humor."

"Yep, thanks." Click.

So, with much prayer for wisdom, I began chapters with, I hope, appropriate humor. For the chapter on the importance of using the "D-word," death, I begin . . .

No one seems to "die" in our culture. They've simply been called home, given up the ghost, returned to dust, gone the way of all mortal flesh, flown to their heavenly reward, crossed over the Jordan, travelled on to Glory, moved up stairs to sing in the heavenly choir.

The less religious are said to be on ice, six feet under pushing up daisies and shoveling coal. Their meter has expired. They've breathed their last, met the Grim Reaper, keeled over, bit the big one, kicked the bucket, bought the farm, cashed in their chips, closed up shop, made the final deadline, went home feet first, shuffled off to Buffalo, and brought down the final curtain. The fat lady has sung and Elvis has left the building.

Actually, they're D-E-A-D!

Funeral director Jim Stone notes, "One of the most important reasons for a funeral is to help the family and friends realize that their loved one has 'died.' Christians do have the hope that the one they love 'has gone to his eternal reward,' but as a funeral director I must help them cope with the fact that the earthly relationship is over."

The basic principles of humor apply to preachers, politicians, and pornographers. But I believe it's the *spirit* in which we write that separates "Christian" humor from all the rest. If we are truly and deeply a Christian, what we write in going to be Christian, whether we mention Jesus or not.

[You can read more about Christian humor in my interview with Al Speegle of *The Wittenburg Door* at http://www.jameswatkins.com/doorinterview.htm.]

4

A funny thing happened on the way to publication

Through humor, you can soften some of the worst blows that life delivers. And once you find laughter, no matter how painful your situation might be, you can survive it.
Bill Cosby

Okay, let's get practical! Here are twenty—count 'em—twenty techniques for your humor tool box.

1. Anecdotes

Erma Bombeck was the queen of anecdotal humor. She also had a royal literary attorney who won't allow me to reprint her work, so here's my less-than-Erma attempt at anecdotal humor.

The Papoose-Driven Life

I consider myself a "purpose-driven" person. I've got a mission statement, an organizer with a calendar, and "to do" list of goals and projects, plus pretty good self-discipline to pull it all off. But when Lois and I babysit three-month-old granddaughter Hannah each Tuesday, forget anything purpose-driven. The day is *"papoose-driven."*

Grandma is not a morning person, so I'm in charge of Hannah the first part of the day. Did I say "in charge" of Hannah? Ha! How delusional. No, the papoose is the chief in the tribe. Occasionally she's asleep when Faith brings her by on her way to work, so I'm able to get some office work done as she sleeps in her car seat by my bookcases.

But once Princess Hannah lets out a war cry, it's time to concentrate on her demands and not my deadlines. I was in the middle of this very column when Hannah awoke and launched one of her infamous WMDs: Weapon-grade Messy Diaper.

I had almost forgotten how the miracle of parenting—and now grand-parenting—makes one immune to the normal revulsion of pooping and puking. Don't put me near someone else's pooping and puking papoose, but it doesn't bother me—too much—when the perpetrator is a part of my own flesh and blood.

Once she has clean diapers, it's time for breakfast and the floor show while the milk is heating. Hannah looks at me as if I've completely lost my mind when I break into my homemade parody of Barry Manilow's "Copacabana":

Her name is Hannah, from Indiana,
The cutest girl north of Havana,
Yes, it's Hannah from Indiana,
In her cabana she's eating bananas.
Yes, it's Hannah, from Indiana . . .

As young as three months, she's learned to roll her eyes just like her mom did as a teen. But my singing provides enough misdirection to keep her occupied until breakfast is served at the precise temperature.

I watch "Good Morning, America" while Hannah enjoys her bottle, but I know my power to determine what programs we watch will soon come to an end. Before I know it, we'll be watching "Teletubbies" and "Barney" because, again, it's a papoose-driven life. "I love you, You love me, I've lost all my sanity!"

Then it's a half-hour play time under her mobile of colorful, plastic fish and an octopus that makes underwater sounds and electronic music. I love it when she smiles, and laughs, and squeals with joy as Grandpa entertains her. But when this ceases to be entertaining, Hannah subtly suggests it's time to go out back to the porch swing by letting out a blood-curdling war cry and turning as red as a drug store Indian. We swing, and swing, and swing some more until she's back to sleep and I can once again become "purpose-driven."

Right now, I'm typing this paragraph while rocking her car seat with my foot. As long as I sit just right so the office chair doesn't squeak and keep my foot moving, I may just have time to finish this column.

Let the record show that I love my granddaughter and am grateful to be able to babysit her once a week.

But I have had to adjust my "purpose-driven" perspective to a "papoose-driven" mindset. On *Survivor* the tribe may speak, but in real world a little squalling squaw has the final decisions. (I'm just thankful that Hannah goes home to her own teepee during the night!)

But there is purpose to this papoose-driven stage: to allow my daughter and son-in-law to use their talents and passions in social work and law enforcement, to have the privilege of influencing this precious little person, to make her laugh with silly songs (I need to find some more words that rhyme with Hannah, though), and to let her know that she's loved unconditionally (even if she's turning red and launching multiple WMDs).

And that is a much greater purpose than writing newspaper columns.

Copyright © 2005 James N. Watkins

Bill Cosby explains his success, first at stand-up and then with the phenomenal *Cosby Show*. "My one rule is to be true rather than funny." George Bernard Shaw would have agreed:

"My way of joking is to tell the truth. It is the funniest joke in the world."

Jean Shepherd also captured universal truth in the classic film *A Christmas Story*. Keep in mind this takes place sometime in the late 1940s, and yet has become a favorite holiday movie since it was release in 1983.

The following lines are my favorites because they resonate so deeply with my own childhood:

Christmas was on its way. Lovely, glorious, beautiful Christmas, upon which the entire kid year revolved.

[On the need for an official Red Ryder, carbine action, two-hundred-shot range model air rifle] Mothers know nothing about creeping marauders burrowing through the snow toward the kitchen where only you—and you alone—stand between your tiny, huddled family and insensate evil.

In the heat of battle my father [actually, *grandfather* in my case] wove a tapestry of obscenities that as far as we know is still hanging in space over Lake Michigan.

He worked in profanity the way other artists might work in oils or clay. It was his true medium; a master.

[On changing a flat tire challenge] Actually the Old Man loved it. He had always pictured himself in the pits of the Indianapolis Speedway in the 500. My old man's spare tires were only actually tires in the academic sense. They were round and had once been made of rubber.

[And who can forget the attack on the turkey by the Bumpis' dogs?] The heavenly aroma still hung in the house. But it was gone, all gone! No turkey! No turkey sandwiches! No turkey salad! No turkey gravy! Turkey Hash! Turkey a la King! Or gallons of turkey soup! Gone,

ALL GONE!

Garrison Keillor (*Lake* Wobegone) and Philip Gulley (*Home to Harmony* series) also capture the truthfulness of small town life with hilarious authenticity. I could see all the parishioners in the church my wife pastored as I read Gulley's books.

And I can certainly relate to Martha Bolton's book, *Didn't My Skin Used to Fit?* She mines the rich ore of reality for those of us over forty:

> I began noticing it several years ago. The skin I had worn for most—no, make that all—of my life suddenly didn't fit anymore. It used to fit. Rather snugly, as a matter of fact. It was tight around the eyes and mouth. There wasn't any extra under my chin or any hanging down from the sides of my cheeks. There was just enough to make one pass around my entire body. One trip was all that was required, and the exact amount was provided to do the job. Not too much, not too little. It was a perfect fit.

Too true! I've noticed my face is sliding off my head and collecting under my chin. If it weren't for my belt, my chest would be around my ankles.

The best anecdotal humor, then, is the unvarnished truth, however people are always asking, "Did that really happen?" You can't make this stuff up!

> It's everyone's worst nightmare. You're speaking in front of a large crowd when you suddenly realize, you're on the platform in just your underwear.
>
> That nightmare came true—only worse—while speaking at a district camp. Because of the short supply of hot water at camp, I had skipped the afternoon service—my first mistake—to take a nice, hot shower. I carefully placed my underwear on the shelf above the sink, before showering. When I returned, I found that some mysterious

force—some would say "divine judgment"—had pushed my skivvies into the sink which unfortunately was plagued with a slow drip. My underwear was soaked. But priding myself as a resourceful person, I wrung them out, laid them on my towel on the shelf, and proceeded to dry them with my blow drier.

So, there I was in Adam's pre-fall condition when the female custodian decided the afternoon service would be a good time to clean the men's rest rooms. Needless to say, we were both shocked and embarrassed. And I never missed another afternoon session!

Or . . .

I don't believe in paying a repair person $50 per hour when I can fix it myself. What do I have to lose? It's already broken, so I really can't do too much more damage.

Such was the case with the "simple"—watch out for that word—task of removing the bathroom stool so the tile crew could install new floor covering. And I'd save $50 by doing it myself!

First, I managed to break the main shut off valve to the house.

No problem, I told myself. *I'll just call the water department to come out and shut off the water for an hour or two.* But then the thirty-year-old bolts magically transformed into little piles of rust when I tried to remove them from the base of the stool.

No problem. I'll just drill them out and run quarter-inch bolts straight through the bathroom floor. This would have worked fine if there had *been* a bathroom floor. A slow leak under the stool had reduced the subflooring to the consistency of wet cardboard.

Faith and Paul seemed to find much about my plumbing predicament to laugh about. "Tim Taylor didn't mess up his bathroom this badly, Dad!" my eight- and twelve-years roared. I had to laugh, too.

Exaggeration

Sid Caesar—who pioneered TV sketch comedy—observed, "Comedy is just truth with a curlicue."

My friend, Rhonda Rhea, wrote a hilarious foreword to my book, *Squeezing Good Out of Bad.* The book deals with top ten ways to react to the lemons of life. Here's an example of her exaggerated anecdote. (At least I *think* she's exaggerating.)

Have you ever lost track of a container or two in the deep recesses of your refrigerator? Just today, I found a lemon in the refrigerator door that had *grown legs.* I didn't even touch that one. Once they're past the tadpole stage, I try not to make them angry. Sometime before the lemon started to walk upright, however, I knew I really had no choice but to wage war against the beast and its assorted furry and fuzzy friends.

It's a good thing putrefying foods have a built-in stench alarm to remind us it's time for a fridge cleaning. There are a few of us who choose to ignore the alarm now and then. It's a courageous move. Extremely dangerous, but courageous. I've heard that if left to themselves for too long, leftovers start forming gangs.

Not too long ago, I found a translucent container hiding under some brown lettuce and a bag of stiff tortillas. I peered through the thing and, horror of horrors, found beefy macaroni. Maybe beefy macaroni doesn't usually horrify you. But when you consider the fact that when I put it in there, I'm pretty sure it was just plain old macaroni, you can understand why I hesitated to open the fridge door unarmed after that. I considered a whip and a chair. Can oven spray wound macaroni? I at least tried to keep a sharp stick handy.

Cleaning the fridge is no small job. You can't grab a

magazine and pull up a chair to start this kind of cleaning process. No, you have to get serious, don some extra heavy rubber gloves and possibly a hazmat suit, stand up, and all but climb in. You have to be strong, stand, and fight.

Now if you'll excuse me, I'm going to take my lemon for a walk. "Heel, boy!"

Relatability

To use anecdotal humor, you have to be able to relate to your readership: age, gender, socio-economic, region, politics, etc. For instance, here's a column that married women may be able to relate to:

Men are dirt

My wife and I can't agree on the definition of "clean."

For instance, I think that cleaning up 99.9 percent of my mustache trimmings from the bathroom sink should earn an "A" for cleanliness. No! One whisker is a D-! And the same for the bathroom mirror. Considering the entire surface area of the mirror (8 square meters), one spot of toothpaste/saliva mixture (0.5 centimeter) would constitute a cleanliness quotient 99.99.

We won't even go into my favorite mug, which Lois is convinced is the source of the West Nile Virus, the recent Anthrax scare, and a possible Ebola outbreak. I think the mug simply has character after several uses.

I suppose it all goes back to Adam and Eve.

"And the Lord God formed man of the dust of the ground, and breathed into his nostrils the breath of life; and man became a living soul. And the Lord God caused a deep sleep to fall upon Adam, and he slept: and he took one of his ribs, and closed up the flesh instead thereof; And the rib, which the Lord God had taken from man, made he a woman, and brought her unto the man."

Simply put, man was created from dirt; while woman was created in some kind of sophisticated, sterile surgical procedure involving genetic engineering.

Thus, there is an inbred instinct that draws boys—of all ages—and dirt together.

This is easily explained by the old law of physics that "nature abhors a vacuum." This law is proven regularly on my desktop. As soon as I have it cleared off, it will attract all kinds of clutter from far reaches of the cosmos (paper clips, Post-It's, Kleenex, junk mail, magazines, coupons, stacks of reference books, computer disks, pens without ink and pencils with broken leads, plus reams of paper covered by a thin layer of pre-formed man). This will continue until the maximum clutter capacity is reached.

In the same way, by cleaning off a five-year-old boy, you are tampering with the forces of nature. This squeaky clean vacuum—that is bathed and dressed in his Sunday best—must be immediately equalized with a like amount of dirt! It's simple physics, people!

This brings us to another undisputed physics principle: The Second Law of Thermodynamics. In a closed system, things degenerate from complex to simple, organized to random, clean to dirty. A house never goes from dusty to sparkling clean, magazines never put themselves away, and laundry never evolves from rancid to "springtime fresh." (This is why the whole notion of evolution is so silly and unscientific.)

My mother, the original Martha Stewart, attempted to defy this law of entropy by cleaning and vacuuming every morning at 6 AM. For some reason, she lived under the delusion that our kitchen was an operating room that must be ready for emergency surgery at a moments notice.

This was during the "Cold War," so perhaps the local Civil Defense unit had designated our house at an emergency M*A*S*H unit. "Excuse me ma'm, but I need to use your kitchen counter to perform a bowel resection!"

Anyway, here's my theory. Men simply take a more scientific, even metaphysical approach to dirt and disorganization than women.

First, since men's basic make-up is "dust to dust, ashes to ashes," they have no aversion to snatching dropped food off the floor ("the five-second rule"), peeing in the shower, or drinking out of a mug that looks like a petri dish from Micro-Biology class. Men are in touch with their inner earth.

Second, clutter and disorganization is a natural, unbreakable law, and no attempt to fight it with magazine racks, closet organizers, or the entire inventory of Rubbermaid will permanently alter the second law of thermodynamics. It's a futile fight. Clutter will win every time!

Note: I should point out that there are subtle ways to alter a male's indifference toward dirt. If hubby wants to enjoy the freshly laundered designer sheets and matching pillow shams with the wife, he can be motivated to make certain concessions on cleanliness. And Lois thinks it's romantic when I empty the dishwasher!

Copyright © 2002 James N. Watkins

When I teach college students, however, I can't use columns on age (I've got socks older than most of them). I can't use my column about my "six pack" turning into a keg (They've got abs of steel; I've got abs of flab.) Know your audience!

5

When the going gets tough . . .
call the urologist

*It's easy being a humorist when you've got
the whole government working for you.*
Will Rogers

2. Associations

One of my favorite types of humor is putting together two activities not usually associated with one another to create a plausible but humorous situation. Here's example from a column in *Rev.* magazine.

Steal or no Steal

"Hi, I'm Howie Mandel and welcome to a special edition of *Deal or No Deal* for church leaders that we're calling *Steal or No Steal*. Tonight, board members can trade in their current small-time pastor for a big-time mega-church pastor. Now, let's bring out our lovely ladies." [dramatic music as lovely ladies march onto stage with cases in hand.]

"Our first contestant is the head of the church board from a small church in Swamp Gas, Louisiana. Welcome, Chuck Roste. Tell a little about yourself."

"Well, I'm chairman of the board of a church of fifteen people with the median age of 65."

"So, trading your current pastor for a new, dynamic pastor would really help out the church."

"Definitely."

"Okay, Chuck, here's how we play this special edition. On the board are twenty potential pastors ranging all the way from, Buck Horne, a 65-year-old pastor of a fifty-member church in Moose Breath, Wyoming, to none other than Joel Osteen, the young, dynamic pastor of Lakewood Church, the largest church in North America with 25,000 in attendance each Sunday. And those same potential pastors' names are in each of the cases our lovely ladies are holding. Select one case, which will be yours, and then we'll begin opening the cases to find out who you didn't select. Periodically, our mysterious district superintendent will phone in to offer to buy your case because he really wants a mega-church pastor in his district. So, Chuck, pick a case."

"Ah, let's try 13, Howie."

"That's the lovely Lisa. Lisa, [dramatic pause] open the case."

PETE MOSS, PASTOR OF HOLY SMOKE ASSEMBLY OF GOD, ATTENDANCE 145.

"Yes, Howie!"

"That's right, Chuck, you still have Joel Osteen on the board, along with Creflo Dollar from College Park with over 23,000 in attendance, Chuck Smith whose Calvary Chapel attracts 20,000, T.D. Jakes with over 18,000 at the Potter's House, and Willow Creek's Bill Hybels with 17,000 in attendance. Pick another case."

"Let's try 4."

"That's the lovely Buffy. Buffy, [dramatic pause] open the case."

RICK WARREN, PASTOR OF SADDLEBACK CHURCH, ATTENDANCE 15,000

"Ouch, Howie!"

"That's okay; the top five pastors are still in play."

[sound of phone] "That's the D.S. with an offer." [serious look] "Okay, I'll tell him. Well, Chuck, you've knocked out Rick Warren, but the D.S. is willing to offer you Robert Schuller whose Crystal Cathedral attracts 4,000 people each Sunday. So, Chuck, [another dramatic pause] 'Steal or no steal?'"

[Audience screams "No steal!"]

"Four thousand?! That's an insulting offer, Howie. You tell the D.S., 'No steal.'"

[Audience cheers]

"Okay, let's open some more cases."

"I'll take 20, Howie."

"That's the lovely Stephanie. Stephanie, [dramatic pause] open the case."

RUSTY NALE, PASTOR OF FIRST NON-DENOMINATIONAL INDEPENDENT COMMUNITY FAMILY CENTER, ATTENDANCE 300

"Yes!"

As game progresses, Chuck knocks out Creflo Dollar, Chuck Smith, and Bill Hybels, but also knocks out more unknown pastors of churches less than 1,000 in attendance. The phone rings. Howie solemnly picks up the phone. "Yes, I know. Okay, I'll tell him. Well, Chuck you've knocked out all of the big names except Joel Osteen. There's a one in two chance that Joel Osteen is in your case, so the D.S. is getting really nervous. He's offering you Betty Peebles who's Jericho City of God regularly has 10,000 in attendance. Ten-thousand is a good offer, Chuck."

[Audience screams "No steal!"]

"No steal, Howie!"

[Audience cheers]

"Okay, Chuck, you're down to two cases. The one you selected and the one the lovely Bambi is holding. You've turned down 10,000, so let's see what is in the case Bambi is holding . . . right after this commercial.

[Commercial]

"We're back. Does Chuck's case contain the name of Joel Osteen or his current pastor? Bambi, [excruciatingly long pause] open the case.

JOEL OLSTEEN, LAKEWOOD CHURCH, ATTENDANCE 25,000

[Audience groans]

"So, Chuck, your case contained your current pastor. What a tough break!"

[Chuck's beeper sounds] "Ah, he just resigned to join Charles Stanley's staff."

[Audience groans] "Sorry, Chuck. We're out of time. Join us next week for our special TV evangelist edition, 'Heal or No Heal?' Goodnight."

Copyright © 2007 James N. Watkins

3. Reverses

This technique takes the reader speeding in one direction and then suddenly makes a 180 degree. The "Tilt-a-Whirl" school of comedy.

For instance here some of my own favorites:

New slogans for old boomers

When the going gets tough, call the urologist
My other car has a handicap sticker
Nothin' says lovin' like something high in fiber
Make a run for the bathroom
Dude, you're getting a pacemaker
Sometimes you feel like a nut, sometimes you feel completely out of your mind
Got Mylanta?
Just for the health benefits of it
Just say 'no' to fudge
A mind is a terrible thing to lose
No pain, no consciousness

Today is the first day of what's left of your life
Shower Naked

Here are some of my favorite reverses from trained professionals:

"Never go to bed mad. Stay up and fight."
Phyllis Diller

"I couldn't wait for success, so I went ahead without it."
Jonathan Winters

"I have a job at the local radio station. I get in my car at rush hour and report on helicopter traffic."
Joe Bolster

Sign at the Bureau of Printing and Engraving: "The buck starts here."

"I have a brother at Harvard Medical School."
"What's he studying?"
"They're studying him."

4. Take-offs

Similar to reverses, take-off start with the familiar, but have a surprising ending—but not necessarily a complete 180 in the intersection. For example . . .

"My father never liked me. For Christmas he gave me a bat. The first time I tried to play ball with it, it flew away." Rodney Dangerfield

"If at first you don't succeed, try, try again. Then quit. No use being a fool about it." W.C. Fields

"I want my children to have all the things I couldn't afford. Then I want to move in with them."

"Aim high, and you won't shoot your foot off."
Phyllis Diller

Here are some examples from a column I wrote each issue in *Rev* magazine—before it went out of business. (It really wasn't my fault! Really!)

Watkins' Church Dictionary

Presenting, the latest entries from the 2009 *Watkins' Church Dictionary:*

Bibull: Sermons that take Scripture out of context.

Carnal nurture: Replacing sermons with motivational talks

Church growth: Side effect of too many carry-in dinners.

Commviction: Psychological technique used to coerce parishioners to serve on church committees.

Deafline: Point pastors pass when their message goes over twenty minutes.

'damentalist: Believer who has lost the "fun" in his/her faith.

Geek Orthodox: A member of an online church.

Ground Zero: youth pastor's office

Heaven's Gate: Senior Bible class.

Helloship: Shallow conversation in church foyers often mislabeled as "fellowship."

Justavacation: Excuses for skipping church

Lite sin: Antonym of "deep sin;" having one-third less disapproval than other leading sins.

McMessage: Entertaining sermon with little nutritional value.

Meology: Self-centered doctrine.

Messchatology: Deriving theology from "last days" novels

Ministry: Suffix, which applied to any activity immediately spiritualizes it (i.e., beach ministry, mall ministry, softball ministry, etc.).

Pew mold: a) globs of gum stuck to the bottom of church seats, or b) person who has been sitting in the same seat, reciting the same testimony, and praying the same prayer for six months or more.

Sinspiration: Motivation to do something right for the wrong reason.

Tele-Vision: Special revelation given to a TV evangelist when contributions fall behind budget projections.

Two-timers: Parishioners who only attend at Christmas and Easter.

Writeousness: Self-righteous attitude of authors who see the speck of dust in their brother's eye, but have a . . . . Uh, sorry, I'm out of room.

*James is a minister in the Wesleyan Church and is married to a pastor of a Friends Church. Does that make them **bisectual***?!

Copyright © 2008 James N. Watkins

A variation of the take-off is when the familiar or cliché comes at the end.

The dog's breath smelled terrible, so his bark *was* worse than his bite.

Sign for tax consultant: HR Block: many happy returns

6

Introducing *The Twitter Bible*

*If you describe things as better than they are, you are considered
to be romantic; if you describe things as worse than they are,
you will be called a realist; and if you describe things exactly
as they are, you will be thought of as a satirist.*
Quentin Crisp

5. Satire

We get the word satire from Greek plays from around 500 BC
called "satyrs" or "satiric dramas." These comedies featured men
dressed as satyrs: the bottom half goat or horse and top half man.
The male goats and horses were—shall we say—"anatomically
correct." Well, actually anatomically *exaggerated*. The bawdy
and explicit comedy sketches were interspersed in serious tragic
plays to provide "comic relief." Satires became so popular, they
developed into full-length plays.

The Romans developed their own brand of satires around 65
BC. The Latin word is *satura* or mixture, literally meaning "dish
of mixed fruit." Rather than sketches, Roman satire tended to be
short verses attacking people and situations with ridicule and
parody. Horace used it in his poetry around 1 BC.

The half goat, half man is a good metaphor. Take a real
situation—a man and a goat—and turn it into a comical situation
by combining the two into a comic creation.

There are basically two forms: one written in "hard news"
form as if it's real (more man than goat) such as *The Onion;* the

other written as obvious parody (more goat than man). *Gulliver's Travels* by Jonathan Swift is a satirical view of the state of European government and of petty differences between religions.

For instance, here's a column I wrote during the impeachment trial of President Clinton:

'The Sound of Monica'

Our team of investigative humor columnists has discovered that backers are being sought for a Broadway musical inspired by the impeachment proceedings against the President.

A reliable cleaning lady at an unidentified theater has provided us access to top secret lyrics for "The Sound of Monica." (A spokesperson for Rodgers and Hammerstein would neither confirm nor deny their involvement in this revision of their popular musical, saying only "They're both dead.")

According to the source, the show opens with Diane Sawyer dancing a top the Hill as she sings . . .

The Hill is alive with the word impeachment,
A song it has sung only twice before,
The Hill is alive with the word impeachment,
But most of the country is already bored
Of Lewinsky and Tripp and their late night chats
and grand juries' sleazy details.
And polls show sixty percent couldn't care
If the law and real justice prevails.

Ken Starr then allegedly sings his version of "My Favorite Things."

Wire taps, subpoenas, and stained dark blue dresses,
Grand juries, inquiries, stolen caresses,

News leaks that spread like the black plague with
wings,
These are a few of my favorite things.

Our source has also produced lead sheets for "Climb Ev'ry Mountain . . . of Evidence" sung by a chorus of White House lawyers.

Mount ev'ry defense, cop ev'ry plea,
Answer ev'ry question with vague legalese.
A case that will try our ideals of justice,
A case to be won for the likes of just us.

According to our source, no one was found to sing the original song "I Must Have Done Something Good."

Also, the decision of who will sing "So Long, Farewell" in the final scene has not been made. Will it be the President? The First Lady? The lawyers? The media? The entire Congress?

Critics, who have also been leaked copies of the script, have panned the production because of its unfinished— and sure to be unsatisfying—ending.

Unlike the original score, there are no clear winners (the good nuns) and losers (the bad Nazis). But perhaps, that is closer to real life than the theater.

No one "wins" wars. One side simply loses less. And as the battle on the Hill escalates, there will be no winners either. The president, the Congress, the media, and the voters are all losers as this long-running production continues in Washington.

So, let's all sing, "I simply remember my favorites things, and then I don't feel so bad." Or better, yet, pray for our President, the Congress, those disillusioned by the scandal, and especially for "that woman, Ms. Lewinky."

I love satire in song, so I posted these ditties during the last election:

Anne Coulter's latest diatribe is called *If Democrats Had Any Brains, They'd Be Republicans*. One could argue, if Republicans had any hearts, they'd be Democrats. Perhaps both parties need to "follow the yellow brick road" for some help from "The Wizard of Oz." Of course, the "Wicked Witch of the Right" and the "Wicked Witch of the Left" will try to stop them as they dance off arm-in-arm to The Emerald City singing . . .

When a man is a conservative,
his logic is superlative
regarding health and art.
Be he mayor or the President
he'd get votes from ev'ry resident
if he only had a heart.
"Vote for me and you will see
some right-winged charity,
Federal aid and programs saved!
If I only had a heart."

When a woman is liberal
emotions are forgivable.
She feels her voters' pain!
Be it judge or the governor
Ev'ryone would simply love her
if she only had a brain.
"Vote for me and you will see
financial sanity,
A strong defense with common sense!
If I only had a brain."

So, this presidential election year, I'm looking for a man or woman who has a brain, a heart and, oh yes, courage!

Parodies

Literary theorist Linda Hutcheon defines parody as work that mocks, comments on, or pokes fun at an original work, its subject or author, or some other target, by means of humorous, satiric or ironic imitation. (To parody the title of literary theorist, I should point out that a) I'm not sure that's even a real title and b) *I* have a PhD in "Para-Linguistics"—but only because my friend, John, bought it from a diploma mill as a Christmas gag gift.)

Here's an example of parody from a column I wrote for *Rev.* magazine.

Introducing *The Twitter Bible*

I was a bit skeptical when, in 1982, *Reader's Digest* offered *The Holy Bible* as one of its condensed books. The Eight Commandments? The ten disciples? The Last Snack? (Actually, by only cutting repetitive texts, they trimmed the Old Testament by 55 percent and the New by 25 percent—with nothing essential missing.)

I'm not sure, however, about the latest Scripture version: *The Twitter Bible.* This investigative humor columnist has obtained these exclusive excerpts:

Had a very good work week, but looking forward to a day of rest. I AM

Feeling really bad. Must have been something we ate. Adam and Eve

I don't think my brother likes me. Abel

The romantic cruise my husband promised turned out

to be a real zoo. Mrs. Noah

We'll be moving. No forwarding address at this time. Abraham

Sleepless night. My hip is killing me. Jacob

Freezing in this prison. This is the SECOND coat I've had ripped off! Joseph

Pharaoh wants to kill my son. I'm a basket case! Jochebed, mother of Moses

I've been out in the desert way too long! Moses

Frog legs for dinner. Again! Pharaoh

What part of "thou shalt not" don't you people understand?! I AM

Looking for new manna recipes. Zipporah

Hebrews are marching around Jericho for the seventh day in a row. Silly Jews! Rahab

No longer following Eliphaz, Bildad and Zophar on Twitter. Job

Played the Palace today. Tough room. David

Nothing interesting happens around here. Think I'll relax in the tub. Bathsheba

A thousand wives? I'm beginning to question my wisdom. King Solomon

Great worship today! Isaiah

Acquired four sharp, young executives in a hostile take-over. King Nebuchadnezzar

Nice kitty. Nice kitty. Daniel

You're not going to believe this fish story! Jonah

Mary, you're what?! Joseph

Wisemen came by the palace asking "Where is the king?" Not a very wise question! Herod

AMBER ALERT! Twelve-year-old male. Last seen at Temple. Joseph and Mary

Herod's wife wants my head. I'm sure it's just a figure of speech. John the Baptist

Follow me. And not just on Twitter! Jesus

Wow! Had a real mountain top experience today! Sons of Thunder

We finally got rid of that trouble-maker Jesus. Caiaphas, high priest

Oops! Caiaphas, high priest

Just signed a real estate deal to die for! Ananias and Saphira

Busy day persecuting Christians. Saul

Busy day being persecuted as a Christian. Paul

Returning soon; can't give exact date and time. Jesus

As the good literary theorist points out, parody doesn't have to lampoon to get laughs. Here's an example:

The Book of Joe

There was a pastor whose name was Joe. He was blameless, upright, feared God, and never lifted his messages from sermons.com without giving proper attribution.

He had two sons and two daughters who never misbehaved in his growing church of two thousand, and he had just been honored as "Pastor of the Year" by his district.

And behold there came a day when Satan appeared before God, and the Lord said to Satan, "Have you considered my servant, Pastor Joe? For there is no pastor like him in all the land for he is blameless, upright, fearing Me, and never turning in his district reports late."

And Satan answered God, "Does Pastor Joe fear God for nothing? Have You not blessed his average attendance figures? But cause his offerings to dip and his secretary to run off with the treasurer—and $100,000—and surely he will curse You to Your face."

And God allowed Satan to test Pastor Joe. And his offerings did dip and his secretary ran off with the treasurer—and $100,000.

Now when three members of the local ministerial association heard of Pastor Joe's troubles, they stopped by his office to comfort him.

And Pastor Joe wept bitterly and said to his friends, "I should have stayed in business school and become an insurance salesman."

And the pastor from the First Church of Divine Potential said to Pastor Joe. "You've got to keep a positive attitude about all this. Don't cave into to negative thinking, but envision a bright future for you and your church. If you just believe it, you can achieve it."

And Pastor Joe wept even more. "But our church is facing scandal and financial ruin."

And the pastor from the Holy Ghost Revival Tabernacle said to Pastor Joe. "Fa-riend, something lucrative is going to happen to you! Jeee-sus is going to pour out the glorious riches of heaven upon you and your church, but first if you'll send your seed faith gift to the Holy Ghost Revival Tabernacle. Then, God will multiply your gift a hundred, a thousand times. Just believe it!"

And Pastor Joe dropped his head on his desk top. "But I do believe."

And the pastor from the Unified Universal Unity Center said to Pastor Joe. "Dude, I'm detecting some really negative energy here. Like, you've got to readjust your reality and envision a positive future. I can see it, man! Offerings are up, your secretary is busy typing up Sunday's bulletin, and the treasurer just discovered an unposted deposit and the church has $100,000 more in the checking account than last reported."

And Pastor Joe said, "I'm going for a walk." And he left His comforters.

As he walked, God spoke through the dust devil spiraling across the church parking lot.

"Who is this that darkens my counsel with words without knowledge? Brace yourself like a man; I will question you, and you shall answer me."

"Where were you when I laid the church's foundation and declared the gates of hell should not prevail against it? Where were you when Rome attempted to wipe out Christianity and the empire crumbled and Christians prevailed? Where were you when the Wesleyan revival saved England from a revolution like the one in France? Where were you there when the Puritans and Pilgrims brought Christianity to America?

"Where were you when the Azusa revival birthed the modern charismatic movement? Where were you when I changed lives at the first Billy Graham crusade in Los Angeles? Where were you when I inspired contemporary Christian music and the Jesus movement? Oh, that's right, you were the one with the peach-fuzz beard and that awful paisley shirt. Sorry."

Then Pastor Joe replied to the Lord, "I know that You can do all things; no plan of Yours can be thwarted. Surely I spoke of things I did not understand, things too wonderful for me to know."

And Pastor Joe returned to his church, and his secretary and treasurer—and $100,000—were still gone—but God was there!

The Whoopee Cushion Code

*I have always noticed that people will
never laugh at anything that is not based on truth.*
Will Rogers

6. Incongruities

I love Andy Rooney's snarky question, "Is there something here I don't understand?" That's the secret to tapping into incongruity. We talked about humor based on revealing incongruities in chapter 1, so keep moving; nothing to see here.

7. Absurdities

This humor genre begins with a logical premise, then adds the absurdity. For instance, most "I Love Lucy" plots began with a logical premise: Lucy wants to get into Ricky's nightclub act or make some extra money. Once the writers had a plausible foundation, they added disguises, working in a chocolate factory, and becoming a spokesperson for "VitaMeataVegaMin."

Here's an example of taking a logical premise (biblical archeology) and adding the absurdity of *The Da Vinci Code* and the other questionable interpretations of history:

The Whoopee Cushion Code

"The Bible is filled with hidden humor." That's the contention of Dr. Harrison "Harry" Tikk, a psychic para-archeologist who claims to have discovered *The Whoopee Cushion Code.* Written on a tanned sheep bladder—thought to be the world's first novelty item—the ancient writing fills in gaps of biblical history with holy humor.

For instance, the document reveals that it was Abraham, speaking to the Pharaoh, who first uttered the classic comedy line, "Take my wife . . . please."

Tikk's discoveries are somewhat controversial, however, in replacing the ten plagues of Egypt with his list of "Top Ten Practical Jokes of All Time" including fake blood, rubber snakes, and windup frogs. And, of course, the Hebrews were the inventors of the dribble flask, clay doo doo, and manna that turned your mouth blue.

Tikk also claims to have decoded Moses' long-lost opening to his great speech from Mount Sinai. (Good speakers always begin with a joke.)

"Hey, how's everybody tonight? Well, 'shofar,' so good (rim shot). So, how 'bout that Passover meal? Great menu if you have to be on the lamb (rim shot). Oy, tough room. I'm dying like firstborn in Egypt (rim shot). Holy smoke, have I got some news for you. . . ."

Prof. Tikk also reveals that Abimelech was not killed by a millstone landing on his head, but with an Acme anvil.

The secret inscriptions also reveal that angels used humor to ease into their pronouncements. For instance, before the angels appeared to the shepherds, Gabriel opened with this, until now, undiscovered monologue.

"I just flew in from heaven, and are my arms tired. Hey, don't be sheep-ish, flock right up here. Ewe'll love the good news I have for you."

In addition to the three wisemen, Tikk argues there were three un-wisemen named Moeshak, Larryshak, and Shemp who brought gold, frankincense and mirth.

The Whoopee Cushion Code reveals its most

controversial claim of all: the rapture is actually a hilarious practical joke. Tikk explains, "It's 'Candid Camera,' 'America's Funniest Home Videos' and 'Punked' all rolled into one."

Here's another example of absurdity. What if Barbie aged? A logical premise (aging) but absurdity (dolls don't age—or talk to reporters).

Barbie turns big 5-0

Fifty years ago this month, Barbie Millicent Roberts emerged from her bright pink box to become the most popular—and at times controversial—doll in the civilized world.

But this investigative humor columnist has discovered gloom beneath the glamour of Mattel's money-making miss.

Wearing faded jeans and a T-shirt, Barbie confided, "I'm just so tired of being dolled up all the time. The whole Barbie image is just so plastic."

In 1967, managers demanded that she undergo plastic surgery for what they called "face sculpting" to create "a new more youthful look." In 1997, Barbie was forced to endure reconstructive surgery for breast reduction and hip enlargement to make her measurements more mainstream. Critics had long argued that her 33-inch bust and 16 1/2-inch waist were an anatomical anomaly—part 22-year old and part 2-year-old.

Despite her objections, Mattel's management has continued to re-invent Barbie. This year tattooed Barbie debuted and, according to secret documents obtained exclusively by this columnist, "Body-piercing Barbie" is planned to celebrate birthday 5-0.

It's so degrading," Barbie confided, "to be viewed simply as a plastic shell. No one cares about who I am inside. Not even Ken!"

The five-decade relationship with Ken has obviously not been satisfying for Barbie. "I'm ready to dump the jerk, hop in my pink Corvette, and drive over to the action figure aisle to find a real man."

Barbie hasn't found satisfaction in a career either. "I've been a fashion model, teacher, an aerobics instructor, ballerina, medical doctor, and over fifty other professions, but I just haven't found satisfaction in any of these careers. I need to find something to fill the hollowness inside. I'm thinking about changing my name to Sister Mary Barbie."

Life has not been any easier for Barbie's siblings who grew up in Willows, Wisconsin. Skipper, who was born in 1964, never attained her older sister's fame and now works as an aid at a doll hospital. The twins Tutti and Todd, born in 1966, have finally found work as stunt doubles for the Pink and Blue Power Ranger action figures. Meanwhile Stacy, introduced in 1992, joined the Air Force but was dishonorably discharged for allegedly having an affair with G.I. Joe. Meanwhile, four-year-old Kelly has not been seen since entering a "Junior Miss Beauty Pageant."

"I just want to sell the dream house, buy a condo in Florida and start acting my age." Although she won't disclose exactly what that age is, she appeared to be in her early 20's when she was introduced in 1959. "Let's just say, I'm way past the 'Hot Flash Barbie' stage in life. And you wouldn't believe the varicose veins you get when you're two-third legs!"

Mattel, which named Barbie and Ken after founders Ruth and Elliot Handler's children, refused to be interviewed in this column, but did release the following statement. "No comment."

Barbie is under contract to Mattel for fifty more years but is hoping to find a way out before the company introduces "Assisted-Living Barbie."

Non sequitur

A *non sequitur* is an illogical statement which is humorous because of juxtaposition of two elements. A classic is Groucho Marx's famous line: "I shot an elephant in my pajamas. How he got in my pajamas, I'll never know."

Yogi Berra, catcher for the Yankees, was the major league master of the *non sequitur*. When asked if his famous "Yogi-isms" were intentional or merely malapropisms, Berra quipped, "I never said most of the things I said." Regardless, here are some of my favorites:

Half the lies they tell about me aren't true.

Ninety percent of this game is half mental.

I always thought that record would stand until it was broken.

If people don't want to come out to the ball park, nobody's gonna stop 'em.

Nobody goes there anymore. It's too crowded.

If you don't know where you are going, you might wind up someplace else.

The future ain't what it used to be.

It's *déjà vu* all over again.

And one of my observations:

I'm worried that my four-year-old granddaughter, Hannah, is dyslexic. She keeps spelling her name backward.

And here's an interesting juxtaposition. Take classic Christian hymns and rewrite them to appeal to the "seeker" audience. (This is a *joke*! Please do *not* use these in your worship service.)

Worship Songs Almost Anyone Can Sing

At Therapy
(Sing to the tune of "At Calvary")
Years I spent with lowest self-esteem
Self-help books on pop psychology,
Knowing there must be a cure for me
At therapy!
Self-acceptance finally came to me,
Free from guilt and shame and self-pity,
There I found A.A. serenity
At therapy!

Love Divine
Love divine, all loves excelling,
Singles groups; dances for teens,
More than bars church is compelling,
For a red hot dating scene.
Singles, divorced, all are welcomed,
Find the love that's, oh so, right!
Visit us on Sunday morning,
Have a date by Friday night.

I Can Sing of Your Love Two Minutes
(Sing to the tune of "I Can Sing of Your Love Forever")
I can sing of your love two minutes (repeat 25 times)

Just As I Ask
(Sing to the tune of "Just As I Am")
Just as I ask, I make this plea
For health and wealth; prosperity

And for all the promises on TV
O Lamb of God, I ask. I ask.

I Love to Give to Missions
(Sing to the tune of "I Love to Tell the Story")
I love to give to missions
It soothes my guilty soul
Of Jesus' commission
Of Jesus' call to "Go"
I love to give to missions,
Because I know it's true,
It's satisfies my calling,
To stay and send out you.

Other possibilities include "Sweet Minute of Prayer," "The Gold-Plated Cross," and "Lord, I Lift Your Name in Vain."

Enjoy!

Copyright © 2006 James N. Watkins

8. Overstatement

Mark Twain wrote, "Get you facts first and then you can always distort them as much as you please." (A side note: I do as much research for my humor column as I do for nonfiction books. For comedy to be taken seriously, you have to be accurate in your writing. Or as Will Rogers noted, "I don't make jokes. I just watch the government and report the facts.")

Melvin Helitzer, who teaches "Humor Writing for Fun and Profit" at Ohio University, explains his "Rubber Band Formula." The shape of the rubber band (realism) is altered. The rubber band is pulled (exaggerated) in different directions by overstatement or understatement. Realism sets up the joke and then—SNAP—goes the exaggeration.

9. Understatement

The English—and my dad—are masters of understatement. One survivor of the German bombing's of London called it, "Rather unpleasant."

In Monty Python's *The Meaning of Life,* death arrives at a dinner party complete with a black robe and scythe. A dinner guest notes, "Well, that's cast rather a gloom over the evening, hasn't it?"

Meanwhile, in *Monty Python and the Holy Grail,* the Black Knight has both arms cut off in a duel and defiantly declares, "It's just a flesh wound."

And in J. D. Salinger's *The Catcher in the Rye,* Holden Caulfield reports, "I have to have this operation. It isn't very serious. I have this tiny little tumor on the brain."

8

If I were any more transparent, I'd be a pane

Comedy is simply a funny way of being serious.
Peter Ustinov

Fifty percent of all humor is based on plays on words, which is good news for those of us who play with words for a living. Here are some types of word plays.

10. Paired phrases/words

To be effective the pair must be parallel and equal in grammar and structure. For instance, you see paired phrases in the most serious of literature:

> He makes me lie down in green pastures,
> he leads me beside quiet waters (Psalm 23:2).

> "Better a witty fool than a foolish wit."
> William Shakespeare

> "Ask not what your country can do for you. Ask what you can do for your country."
> John F. Kennedy

> "If guns are outlawed, only outlaws will have guns."
> National Rifle Association

Like paired phrases, individual words can be paired:

It's difficult to act youthful without acting childish.

She wasn't just throwing herself at him. She was taking careful aim.

"The kind of humor I like is the thing that makes me laugh for five seconds and think for five minutes."
William Davis

11. Double Entendre
Double entendres are ambiguous words or phrases that allow for a double interpretation of words:

"The patient refused the transplant saying he'd had a change of heart."
George Carlin

My son and I, attending a wedding were asked by the usher if we were on the groom's side or the bride's side. My son was shocked.
"Are they taking sides already?"
Lillian Koslover

Oxymorons also fall under this category. The name comes from the Greek words for sharp and dull. Here are some of my favorites: resident alien, airline food, government intelligence, sanitary landfill, legally drunk, living dead, political science, pretty ugly, rap music, and Microsoft Works.
Oxymoronic phrases can be a great source of humor:

Some people say that I'm superficial, but that's just on the surface.

If there's one thing I can't stand, it's intolerance.

Prejudiced people are all alike.

I'm still not sure if I understand ambiguity.

One should never generalize.

Exaggeration is a billion times worse than understatement.

An oral contract isn't worth the paper it's written on.

Free advice is worth what you paid for it.

There are only three kinds of people; people who can count and people who can't.

12. Single entendre?

I suppose the opposite of double entendre would be, well, a single entendre—taking the literal meaning. Here are some examples:

"Why do you park in driveways and drive on parkways?"
Steven Wright

"My wife went window shopping yesterday and came home with seven windows."
Rodney Dangerfield

"Thank you for sending me a copy of your book. I shall waste no time reading it."
Benjamin Disraeli

My favorite example, though, occurred while I was in a desperate battle with a shelving unit. I asked my son, Paul, who was five at the time to please get me a yardstick to square it up.

Five minutes and one headache later, I heard rustling coming down the hall. I turned to see Paul dragging half a tree.

"Paul, I said a *yardstick*."

"But Dad," he said innocently, "it was the biggest stick in the yard." I let the shelving unit collapse and had a great time laughing and hugging with my son.

13. Reforming

Aristotle wrote about the power of metaphors to produce a surprise in the hearer. "The effect is produced even by jokes depending upon changes of the letters of a word; this too is a surprise. You find this in verse as well as in prose. The word which comes is not what the hearer imagined."

By altering one or two letters or changing the spelling, you can create humor.

Homonyms work best in print. Here are a couple of mine:

If I were any more transparent, I'd be a pane.

I've worked in both staff and staph ministries. One is a group of people working together well; the other is a painful irritation.

Puns can be tricky. I've dubbed one of my friends as "The Pun-isher." Occasionally his puns are brilliant, but most of the time his puns are only 66.6 percent there: PU!

You decide which of these pun-liners are actually pun-ny.

A bicycle can't stand alone; it is two tired.

A will is a dead giveaway.

If you don't pay your exorcist you can get repossessed.

He would often have to break into song because he couldn't find the key.

A calendar's days are numbered.

He had a photographic memory which was never developed.

A plateau is a high form of flattery.

Those who get too big for their britches will be exposed in the end.

Santa's helpers are subordinate clauses.

Verb choice can be a great source of humor. For instance, an angry firefighter would be burned up about something. A firefighter's compliment could include "Smokin'" or "That's hot!"
Some other examples:

"Make a canoe of that tree," he barked.

"It's a dog's life," he muttered.

"The faucet's broken," she gushed.

"I wish I were back in the forest," she pined.

And one of my favorite Rhonda Rhea lines:

I feel like I might be coming down with kleptomania. I hope there's something I can take for it.

Adverb choice works the same way:

"The smog is really bad today," he cried breathlessly.

"My feet hurt," Tom said flatly.

"I'm hot!" the firefighter fumed.

Antonyms

Go with the opposite. For instance, critics of the recent SNL called it "Saturday Night Dead."

"Your manuscript is both good and original, but the part that is good is not original and that part that is original is not good."
Attributed to Samuel Johnson

"I bought a humidifier and a dehumidifier. I put them in the same room and let 'em fight it out."
Steven Wright

14. Triplets

In serious and silly writing there is power in threes. Throughout the Bible there are "Father, Son, Holy Spirit," "gold, frankincense and myrrh," and "faith, hope and love."

The Declaration of Independence promises "life, liberty and the pursuit of happiness."

Abraham Lincoln's used triplets with his famous "of the people, by the people, for the people."

And so in humor, you have "Three Stooges," "A minister, a priest and a rabbi walk into a bar. . . ."

Triplets are also used in longer pieces. Here's how most humor triplets work:

Preparation (set up the situation)
Anticipation (triple)
Punch line (story payoff)

Henry Youngman, most famous for "Take my wife . . . please," offers this great triplet:

Preparation: The reason my wife and I have been happily married for forty years is because we go out to dinner once a week.
Anticipation: Some candlelight, a little wine, soft music.
Punch line: I go out on Friday night, she goes out on Saturday.

And the famous "How many people does it take to change a light bulb?" is also based on triplets. Here's the three-part formula:

One to: hold the ladder
One to: one to screw in the bulb
(Punch line) "And [number] to [fill in the blank]

So, how many government employees does it take to change a light bulb?

Fifty-two. One to hold the ladder, one to screw in the bulb, and fifty to draft the environmental impact study.

Three phrases or lines also work well. Lily Tomlin as, "If peanut oil comes from peanuts, and olive oil comes from olives, where does baby oil come from?" Lily Tomlin

15. Funny words

In Neil Simon's play, *The Sunshine Boys*, Willy tells his nephew:

Fifty-seven years in this business, you learn a few things. You know what words are funny and which words are not funny. Alka Seltzer is funny. You say "Alka Seltzer" you get a laugh . . . Words with "k" in them are funny. Casey Stengel, that's a funny name. Robert Taylor is not funny. Cupcake is funny. Tomato is not funny. Cookie is funny. Cucumber is funny. Car keys. Cleveland

. . . Cleveland is funny. Maryland is not funny. Then, there's chicken. Chicken is funny. Pickle is funny.

9

'That would make a great name for a rock band'

I'm not making this up!
Dave Barry

16. Running gags

Pulitzer-winning humorist Dave Barry was the master of running gags throughout his weekly columns. Here's an excerpt from a newspaper column I wrote when Dave announced he was going on a sabbatical—and I promptly went into a deep depression. This portion addresses his running gags.

Alert readers

"Alert readers" are constantly sending Barry outrageous news and news headlines. Just recently Melba Glock sent in a story from the *Lincoln Journal Star* headlined: "Volunteers needed to help torture survivors."

Frank Florio sent an obituary-page announcement from the *Watertown Times* that reads, "To Everyone and Anyone who was in any way involved in my husband's passing, a Heart Felt Thank You."

And Susan Anderson sent an item from the *Fort Myers News-Press* headlined "Homeless man improves after car runs into him."

Great names for rock bands

Barry is constantly skewering pompous sounding government programs, medical procedures, and, oh, whatever with "That would be a great name for a rock band." Examples include "Low-Flow Toilets," "The Flaming Booty Moths," and "Hanging Chads." Alert reader Chuck Goodman notes there's an actual group called "Throbbing Gristle."

Mottos

Some of my favorite Barry mottos include:

U.S. Food and Drug Administration: "We Have Not Yet Determined That Our Motto Is Safe."

Alaska: "Brrrrrrr!"

Champaign, Ill.: "Gateway to a Whole Lot Of Flatness."

Washington, D.C.: "Don't Laugh: You're Paying for It."

And Miami's official tourism slogan: "Maybe You Won't Get Shot"

Mr. Language Person . . .

I'll also miss "Mr. Language Person," "The Year in Review," and the annual "Christmas Shopping Guide" ("toilet bowl decals" anyone?). I just discovered that amazon.com is selling—and I'm not making this up—home defibrillators. Now that would be a great name for a rock band!

And of course Barry's trademark, "I'm not making this up!" Man, I miss Dave Barry's weekly columns!

17. Toppers

Here's my attempt at "topper," which is a follow-up joke based on the first joke:

First: I'm on a first-name basis with the Pope.
Second: Yeah, well I'm a first-name basis with Jesus.
First: Funny, but I don't know you.

The reader thinks the joke is done and then—SURPRISE—another!

10

The doctor spanked my umbilical cord and tied me in knot

The wit makes fun of other persons; the satirist makes fun f the world; the humorist makes fun of himself.
James Thurber

18. Self-deprecation

I had the privilege of rummaging through the manuscript critique files at the Mount Hermon Christian Writers' Conference and discovering one of the funniest writers—ever. I immediately took it to an editor and said, "You've got to sign this guy." David Meurer is now a popular book and article author. His goal is to "tell the truth, teach a few serious concepts, and make people laugh so hard that they almost commit a hygienic lapse." He explains how he does this with self-deprecating humor:

> If you pick up one of my books you will immediately notice that virtually all the humor is at my expense. I am the butt of the jokes. Even when it seems like I am poking fun at someone else, it ends up with me looking like the oaf. I let my wife and kids review my material, and it has to pass muster with them or it does not get printed. I have read material by other people who seem to cross that line and make fun of others. I never find it funny, and I don't

want to do it. If you think I cross that line, please let me know. Seriously.

And here's an example from Dave's Web site:

If you are a rational, thoughtful, wise person, I have to assume that you have reached my Web site due to simple human error or some kind of catastrophic failure in your search engine. It can't be because you are actually seeking out my material, because the rational, thoughtful, wise people are reading Phil Yancey and William Shakespeare and C.S. Lewis and Peanuts cartoons. Or could it be that you have just been *pretending* to be all sophisticated and discerning and astute while you have quietly been reading my stuff, and you are hungry for even more? Is *that* it? If you have truly stooped that low, well, join the club!

Once when Abraham Lincoln was accused of being "two-faced," he replied, "If I had two faces, would I be wearing this one?"

With self-deprecation, you can get away with all kinds of jokes about your gender, your race, your religion—without being accused of being sexist, racist, or the anti-Christ.

For instance, here's a sample of what would be considered sexist if written by a woman, but as a self-deprecating male, I can get away with it—I think:

Testosterone poisoning: why guys do what guys do

If you're in any kind of relationships with carbon-based life forms of the opposite gender, you've already figured out there's a big difference between you and them.

And it goes way beyond those health class movies from junior high! John Gray may believe that *Men are from Mars, Women are from Venus*, but they're from two separate galaxies "far, far away."

This research paper attempts to help those with "XX" and "XY" chromosomes understand the delightful—and disturbing—differences between the genders.

Here at The Watkins Polytechnic Institute for the Research of Love, Sex, and Male-Pattern Blindness, we've made some startling observations concerning Hormonal Output Toxicity Syndrome (HOTS for short).

For instance, the male hormone testosterone contributes to the competitive, aggressive nature of the male and may explain some of the following contradictory behaviors:

Men subjects exhibit "Male-Pattern Blindness" in which the victim can spot a '69 Corvette at a mile and a half, but can't see the ketchup in the refrigerator.

Some researchers speculate that, because early man was a hunter, males have adapted incredible ability to see prey at great distances. For instance, Native American civilization could continue only if Chief Running Water and his braves could spot dinner at a mile and a half. It was not, however, essential for survival to find his clean buckskins. Thus, the law of survival of the fittest, has produced males with highly discriminating vision—able to see buffalo, sports cars, and hardware stores at incredible distances, but oblivious to water rings on coffee tables, an inch of dust on their desks, or bills that were over-due last week.

Another annoyance is that males tend to possess long-range sight, but extremely short-range patience. Thus, if the subject has not found something within a few micro-seconds, he resorts to whining, "Where are my bow and arrows?" This brings us to a companion corollary . . .

Males suffering from HOTS, while admitting they can't find their clean socks in their own home, refuse to stop for directions while searching for Ralph's Reptile Reserve ten states away! Male researchers are stumped.

(Perhaps, because they refuse to ask why this is happening.)

Others claim that men have tiny deposits of iron at the base of the nose which act as a compass, so that males instinctively know when they are facing north. Of course, this does no good if they don't know if Ralph's is to the west or east.

Studies also reveal that male victims can display sophisticated sensory motor skills such as picking up a 7-10 split at the bowling alley, but seem incapable of picking up their dirty socks at home. The competitive nature produced by testosterone causes men to love challenges (and to be obnoxious board game players). But quite frankly, picking up dirty clothes doesn't qualify as a challenge worthy of their finely honed athletic skills.

Finally figuring this out, a friend of my wife's installed a toy basketball rim over the clothes hamper. Her two "children" (ages three and twenty-five), now enjoy slam-dunking their skivvies and going for three-point shots with their socks.

The secret, then, is to make every task a challenge. "Honey, we need milk. But . . . I don't know . . . the car's making a funny noise, there's a lot of traffic out there, and you know how obnoxious that clerk at Quickie-Mart can be. Maybe you better not." He's changed the spark plugs faster than an Indy pit crew and is speeding through rush-hour traffic to do battle with "Vermin" the clerk!

Copyright © 1990 James N. Watkins.

Here are a couple of my own self-deprecating one-liners:

I was so skinny, the doctor spanked my umbilical cord and tied me in knot.

As a teen, I had acne and braces. I looked like a pepperoni pizza with a zipper.

I've tried it, but I'm just no good at self-deprecation.

And some from trained professionals:

"I cannot sing, dance or act; what else would I be but a talk show host."
"Let me just say a word about these jokes that I am telling right now, ladies and gentlemen. Like President-elect Obama says, 'It's going to get worse before it gets better."
"I know these jokes aren't great, ladies and gentlemen, see this is the problem you run into when you're between impeachments."
David Letterman

"I am my own blooper reel, as it happens."
Craig Ferguson, host of "The Late, Late Show," who constantly admits his amazement that people are actually watching "this lame crap."

"Most people get an appointment at a beauty parlor. I was committed!"
"I spent seven hours in a beauty shop—and that was for the estimate."
"It's a good thing that beauty is only skin deep, or I'd be rotten to the core."
Phyllis Diller

Others with an appreciation for deprecation include Conan O'Brien, Jon Stewart, and Woody Allen.
And self-deprecation may be the only comedy technique that comes with a biblical promise:

"But those who exalt themselves will be humbled, and those who humble themselves will be exalted" (Matthew 23:12).

So humble yourselves under the mighty power of God, and at the right time he will lift you up in honor (1 Peter 5:6).

Two forms of humor, to me, don't belong in the Christian's comedy tool box.

19. Insults

This comedy form doesn't fit the greatest commandment (to love God and our readers), the golden rule (to tell jokes about others as you would have them tell jokes about you), the command to let our conversations be full of grace (Colossians 4),

20. Shock/obscenity

[Bleep] it! It takes no [bleep, bleeping] creativity or [bleep, bleeping] skill to attempt a laugh using [bleep, bleeping] humor.

11

Timing is *almost* everything

*A man's got to take a lot of punishment to write
a really funny book.*
Ernest Hemmingway

You now have a comedy tool box filled with humor techniques, but apparently, some people need specific instructions how to use tools. For instance, these actual instructions on tools and appliances:

"Warning: Never iron clothes on the body."

"Do not use in shower." "Do not use while sleeping." On hair dryer.

"This product not intended for use as a dental drill." On electric rotary tool.

"Do not use for drying pets." On microwave oven.

"May be harmful if swallowed." On shipment of hammers.

"Turn off motor before using this product." On chainsaw file.

"Do not attempt to stop blade with hand." On chainsaw.

So, as a public services—and to prevent you for suing me for unauthorized uses of this book—here are some instructions for using humor safely and effectively:

Put the punch line *last*

Okay, that's almost as ridiculous as telling you not to iron your clothes while wearing them, but I find myself occasionally not putting the punch in the *very* last position.

For instance, which is funnier, A, B, or C? ("None" is not an option!)

A: I'm critically acclaimed, but commercially ashamed since my books have won awards, but never a spot on the best-seller lists.

B: My books have won awards, but never a spot on the best-seller lists. I'm commercially ashamed but critically acclaimed.

C: My books have won awards, but never a spot on the best-seller lists. I'm critically acclaimed, but commercially ashamed.

A gives away the punch line and B fails to put the funniest phrase very last. So, C is the winner.

Use details

Here's another pop quiz. In my column on intolerance (see chapter 1). Which is funnier? A or B? (Again, "neither" is incorrect!)

A: For instance, do you really want to go to a "tolerant" doctor? I want a doctor who is narrow-minded and completely intolerant to disease.

B: For instance, do you really want to go to an "open-minded" doctor with signs in the waiting room that read: "I Brake for Bacteria," "Save the Salmonella," or "Take a Stand for Polio"?! I want a doctor who is narrow-minded and completely intolerant to disease and physical afflictions when I'm told, "Turn your head and cough."

The secret is in the details!

Work on your timing

Timing is the secret to "stand up" and "sit down" comedy, so be sure you read your article aloud. Or, better yet, have someone in your writing critique group read it aloud. This allows you to hear it as the reader is actually hearing it.

Listen closely for the timing. Did you take too long to set up the joke? Did you rush the telling?

Read other humorists

Some of my favorites are sprinkled throughout the book: Dave Barry, Erma Bombeck (*Forever Erma* is a wonderful tribute of her best columns), Patsy Clairmont, Philip Gulley, Barabara Johnson, David Muir, Rhonda Rhea, Laura Jensen Walker, etc.

And, whatever you do, don't use your hair dryer in the shower!

12

Listening to the voices in your head

Writing is a socially acceptable form of schizophrenia.
E. L. Doctorow

There are at least three things you'll hear in every writing class:

Show don't tell.
Write tight.
Develop your own voice.

Several years ago, I was asked to write a book review for *Leadership,* which is a very scholarly, academic journal for ministers. So, I wrote a very scholarly, academic review. The editor wrote back, "Jim, we love your irreverent style. Lighten up!"

So it's important to discover your writing voice. It's the way your writing "sounds." Is it friendly, formal, chatty, distant?

I won a *Campus Life* "Book of the Year" award for *Death & Beyond.* It was an especially meaningful honor because the student readers themselves did the judging. One girl wrote, "Jim is not an author." (Teens can be so cruel!) She went on to say, "No, it's like he's sitting across from you at McDonald's sharing Diet Cokes." (Okay, I can live with that.)

With humor writing, most have a voice and a "character." Here are some examples:

The underdog, down-trodden
Rodney Dangerfield made a whole career—and a lot of money—simply noting that he got "no respect."

I asked my old man if I could go ice-skating on the lake. He told me, "Wait till it gets warmer."

When I was a kid I got no respect. The time I was kidnapped, and the kidnappers sent my parents a note they said, "We want five thousand dollars or you'll see your kid again."

I went to my psychiatrist and I said, "Doc, I have this terrible feeling people are trying to take advantage of me."
He say's, "Relax. Everyone thinks someone is trying to take advantage of them."
"Gee, thanks, Doc. How much do I owe you?"
He says, "How much do you have?"

Gary Shandling, Jackie Gleason also made careers out being successful "failures."

The intellectual, the nerd
Woody Allen has used this character successfully, first in standup and then in his films.

I don't want to achieve immortality through my work. I want to achieve it through not dying.

It's not that I'm afraid to die. I just don't want to be there when it happens.

Death should not be seen as the end, but as a very effective way to cut down expenses.

On the plus side, death is one of the few things that can done just as easily lying down.

Steven Wright has also based his career on clever, intellectual humor:

What happens if you get scared half to death twice?

I used to have an open mind but my brains kept falling out.

If you had a million Shakespeares, could they write like a monkey?

I put instant coffee in a microwave oven. I almost went back in time.

Political/social commentator

Jay Leno, Jon Stewart, and Dave Barry tend to be political and social commentators. (Barry actually won a Pulitzer for political commentary). Here are few of my favorite Stephen Colbert comments:

I stand by [the President] because he stands for things. Not only for things, he stands on things. Things like aircraft carriers, and rubble, and recently flooded city squares. And that sends a strong message that no matter what happens to America she will always rebound with the most powerfully staged photo-ops in the world."

When the president decides something on Monday, he still believes it on Wednesday — no matter what happened Tuesday.

And although Will Rogers died in 1935, his commentary is still incredibly relevant:

A fool and his money are soon elected.

Alexander Hamilton started the U.S. Treasury with nothing, and that was the closest our country has ever been to being even.

The only difference between death and taxes is that death doesn't get worse every time Congress meets.

I am not a member of any organized political party. I am a Democrat.

My tag line is "Heavy topics with a light touch," so I suppose I fall into this category. I write about everything from sex to sects. (Check out www.jameswatkins.com.)

Storytellers

Mark Twain, Garrison Keillor (*A Prairie Home Companion* radio show, books), Jean Shepherd (*A Christmas Story*), and Bill Cosby are master story-tellers.

My friend, Torry Martin, is a brilliant comic storyteller. (He's also an award winning actor, author and comedian who currently writes for *Adventures in Odyssey*, the popular radio program.) Here's one of his famous "Torry Stories."

A Complete Ensemble

Shortly after moving from Washington State to California to attend college, I decided I needed to go shopping for some new shorts. I was down to only one pair, and they were quickly becoming recognizable to the other students on the Vanguard University campus.

Apparently everyone else in Costa Mesa knew that shorts and a T-shirt are the Southern California uniform but what they neglected to mention was that I needed to have more than just one set of them when I arrived. As a college student I didn't have a lot of money and I wasn't very fond of shopping either but with grim determination I forced myself to open my billfold wallet and the door to the mall in an effort to rectify my fashion *faux pas*. When I happened upon a sidewalk sale and discovered numerous pairs of shorts in my size, I was elated. I grabbed about ten pairs and began trying them on in the dressing room. About five pairs fit, so I took both bundles up to the check out counter.

"I'd like to buy all of these," I told the clerk as I handed him the stack of shorts that I wanted to buy. "And you can have these," I said, handing him the second stack of shorts, the ones I didn't want.

"You don't want any of these?" he asked, looking over the rejected stack.

"No. Just those five I've picked out," I said.

"You're sure?" he pressed.

"I'm sure," I said, wondering why he was being so pushy. I was buying five pairs of shorts. Wasn't that enough? Was he working on a quota system or something?

"You're really sure these are all you want?" he continued.

"Yes," I said emphatically. "These are the only ones I want."

I could feel the veins in my neck beginning to bulge.

"All right," he said as he began to ring them up. "I just thought you might like to take these," he said, holding up the pair of shorts I had worn into the store. I didn't even want to look down. I knew at that instant I was standing there in my underwear and T-shirt. I grabbed my shorts and rushed back to the dressing room to finish dressing. California's casual, but not that casual!

[Read more at www.torrymartin.com.]

Country bumpkin, redneck

Jeff Foxworthy, Red Green, and Larry the Cable Guy have done very well with this persona. Foxworthy is probably most famous for "You might be a redneck if. . . .

You think the last words to "The Star Spangled Banner" are "Gentlemen, start your engines."

You've been married three times and still have the same in-laws.

Your house still has the "WIDE LOAD" sign on the back.

Skits-ophrenic

Some of us have multiple characters running around inside our little heads, so we have to resort to comic sketches. Here's one of my favorites:

Brother Bob Blessing

Brother Bob: Ain't God great! Hi, fa-riend, I'm Brother Bob Blessing here with another exciting special: "Something Lucrative is Going to Happen to You!" Behind me is the beautiful billion-dollar "Ain't God Great Center"—home of our satellite TV station, the "Ain't God Great Radio Network," our seven-thousand-seat auditorium and fitness center, and of course our "Springs of Blessings" water slide. From here we proclaim the good news the world is waiting to hear: "Jesus wants you healthy and wealthy." We'll be telling how you can be blessed by sharing in this exciting ministry in just a moment. But first friend, let me introduce today's co-host. He's assertive. He's positive. He's one of Christ's own disciples. Here he is, your favorite disciple and mine . . . Saint Peter!

[Saint Peter enters, appearing overwhelmed by the sets, lights and cameras.]

Brother Bob: Welcome to our "Something Lucrative is Going to Happen to You" special, Saint Peter.

Peter: You can just call me Peter.

Brother Bob: Well, what an honor to meet one so positive and assertive, and of course, healthy and wealthy.

Peter: Well, actually I've got this really bad cold I picked up in prison and I'm afraid I don't have any silver or gold.

Brother Bob: [talking to off-stage]: Keep the tape rolling, Nick, but make a note to edit that out in production. You see, Peter, I'm Brother Bob Blessing—the world's most positive thinker. Jesus wants us healthy and wealthy. We're King's kids. Ah, let's try another approach. Take two. Five. Four. Three. Two. [silently count "one"] Peter, you were one of Christ's closest friends. What positive and powerful message stands out above all the others.

Peter: I guess the Sermon on the Mount. Jesus started out by saying, "Blessed are the poor in spirit, for theirs is the kingdom of . . .

Brother Bob: Cut! Peter, you don't seem to understand that this is a positive show. God doesn't want us living below our privileges. He loves you and has a wonderful Porche for your life. [Talking to off-stage] Roll the tape, Nick. Take three. Five. Four. Three. Two. [pause] One of Christ's messages that stands out to Saint Peter is the Sermon on the Mount.

Peter: "Blessed are those who mourn, for they shall be comforted."

Brother Bob: Cut! What do you mean "mourn." If you think on positive things, if you really believe that something lucrative is going to happen to you, then life can be continuously happy.

Peter: But I get beat up everywhere I go sharing the Gospel. And my close friend, James, was beheaded. And worse than that, there are people dying this moment and going into eternity without Christ.

Brother Bob: Just don't think about it, fa-riend. Fill your mind with positive thoughts. [To off-stage] Keep the tape rolling, Nick. We may be able to salvage some of this. [To Peter] Please, say something positive.

Peter: Well, I'm basically a "go for it," assertive and confident sort of guy . . .

Brother Bob: Pa-raise God! Yes, fa-riends, it's those who assert themselves and name it and claim it that the Lord blesses.

Peter: . . . but I've learned that only the meek will inherit the earth.

Brother Bob: [To off-stage] Make a note to edit that out. Take four. Five. Four. Three. Two. [pause] [To Peter] Is there *anything* positive you remember Christ saying?

Peter: Oh, sure. Most of it.

Brother Bob: Finally! Peter remembers Christ as someone who thought positively, lived positively, and was positively successful! Can you share some of those thoughts, Peter?

Peter: Sure, "Blessed are those who hunger and thirst for righteousness, for they will be filled."

Brother Bob: Pa-raise the Lord! Thank you Jeee-sus! Yes, Jeee-sus want to fill our lives to overflowing!

Peter: "Blessed are the merciful, for they will be shown mercy."

Brother Bob: Pa-reach it, friend!

Peter: "Blessed are the pure in heart, for they shall see God."

Brother Bob: Hallelujah!

Peter: "Blessed are the peacemakers, for they will be called children of God."

Brother Bob: Ga-lory! Yes, friends, God wants you to be His son or daughter and experience all His riches. Just dial 1-800-BLESSED and . . .

Peter: "Blessed are those who are persecuted because of righteousness for theirs is the kingdom of . . .

Brother Bob: CUT!

Peter: "Blessed are you when people insult you and falsely say all kinds of evil against you . . . .

Brother Bob: Okay, that's enough! Are the mikes off? Look, Peter, it's been great being with you, but—nothing personal—you're not the kind of guest this special needs.

[Peter walks off shaking his head.]

Brother Bob: [To off-stage]: Nick, see if you can get me the disciple who wrote "God's divine power has given us everything we need for life and godliness." [pause as if Nick answers Brother Bob] That *was* him?!

[Brother Bob walks off shaking his head.]
Copyright © 1982 James N. Watkins

Worldly characters

Some characters that probably won't work in the Christian market: **Drug-crazed anarchist** (George Carlin's early years, Richard Pryor), **the jerk, the insulter** (Ron Rickels, Triumph the Insult Dog), **the racist** (Archy Bunker), etc.

The secret to voice and character is to be authentic to who you are.

13

'You had to be there'

*You may be very funny sitting and talking to your friends
but there's a definite craft involved in taking strangers and
getting them through something that you've written
in a way that they find it to be amusing.*
Dave Barry

From stand-up to sit-down comedy

The spoken word and the written word are two very different animals. They're both forms of communication but that's like saying, in the cat family, you have Siamese kittens and Saber Tooth tigers. They're both cats, but *very* different cat-egories.

So, let's look at the differences between speaking and writing, seek out the similarities, and provide some practical ways to go from the stage to the page . . .

First . . . the differences.

On the stage

Whether it's on stage or in the office break room, you have a variety of items in your comedy tool box.

You have your voice (which makes up 30 percent of our communication). It's a wonderful, versatile tool that includes tone of voice, volume, and melodic quality.

I'm not talking about words, but the actual vibration of vocal chords. For instance, Tim Allen's *Home Improvement* made a sophisticated form of communication from merely grunting.

You have your body language (which makes up over 50 percent of your communications) such as gestures and facial expressions. Did your Mom or Dad have "the look"? You're cutting up in church, and they just have to give you the look for you to know you'll be spending Sunday afternoon in your room.

Body movements such as arms firmly crossed (disagreement) or arms open (acceptance) convey distinct messages.

You have props. In the local parish, I used lots of props in my messages. I rode down the aisle on a bicycle with a white shirt and black pants and gave a message as if I was a Mormon "missionary" to point out the unbiblical tenets of the religion.

I spoke from Philippians 3 about everything being trash compared to knowing Christ so would put something in a trash can to make point:

T-itles (ordination certificate)

R-iches (my brand new Godin guitar)

A-ccomplishments (*Campus Life* award plaque)

S-holarship (transcript from grad school)

H-oliness (a book I wrote on avoiding legalistic holiness)

And one Sunday, I made waffles on the platform as I talked about political and spiritual "waffling."

And, of course, you have . . .

Words, but they make up only 10 percent of our daily conversation. Hmmm?

On the page

But when you open your writer's tool box, there's no voice, no body language, no props. Nothing but written words! You've gone from the stage's 100 percent effect down to 10 percent: black ink on white paper or pixels on a computer screen.

That's why simply transcribing a speech or stand-up routine never works. You lose 90 percent of the effect!

On the stage, you're in front of the audience; in writing, you're in front of a computer screen.

You're probably known as a speaker or comic to friends, colleagues, or congregants. There's a relationship there: you know them, they know you; you both know the appropriate behaviors for that setting.

In writing, you may not have a relationship with your readers. They're reading a magazine and come upon your article, or they're surfing the Web and happen to click on your site. How are you going to connect with your readers?

Developing rapport with people you've never met

Here are some ways:

Get sample copies of the magazine.

Read the writer's guide.

At the teen magazine I edited for six year, we had surveyed youth camps in our denomination. We knew exactly who our reader was:

> Jennifer is fifteen years old, a Christian, and attends church and youth meetings faithfully. She doesn't have a regular time alone with God and rarely reads her Bible. A good friend has tried sex and drugs, but she hasn't. She has a crush on a guy at church, but he acts like she doesn't exist. She has no convictions against dating a non-Christian, but is not sure where she stands about marrying a non-Christian.

So, as I dug through the pile of unsolicited manuscripts on my desk, I was only interested in articles that would effectively communicate with Jennifer.

All magazines have "writers guidelines" that provide detailed information on their readers.

In person, your audience probably knows you and trusts you as a speaker or they'd never let you near a lectern or pulpit. People are going to believe what you say because you have a history with the audience.

Hopefully, in writing, the magazine is an old friend. They've been subscribing to it for years. Or, the reader trusts the book publisher. When you write for denominational houses, they really run the author through the theological gauntlet. One publisher actually has an editorial committee, marketing committee *and* doctrinal committee!

Honesty and transparency are two important tools to connect with your reading audience. Remember the chapter on the power of humor to build rapport. But without honesty and transparency, you're not going to connect.

Ernest Hemmingway wrote that a good writer has a good—and I'm paraphrasing—"doo doo" detector. He or is not false in anyway. I think readers have an even more powerful doo doo detector.

So honesty and transparency earn you credibility. That's probably the reason Ann Lamott is popular in both Christian and general markets. She is incredibly honest and transparent—although I wish she would sanctify her [bleeping] vocabulary!

Gaining feedback from readers you can't hear

I love speaking to black audiences because they talk right back: "That's right." "Uh huh." "You preach it." You get into the rhythm like you're playing tennis. You serve an idea, and—PING—they return the ball.

With any group, you're receiving feedback—"yahs" to yawns, applause to produce—so you can quickly adapt your presentation by picking up or slowing down the tempo, explaining a point that's eliciting looks of confusion, or skipping minor points to quickly conclude. (If you haven't struck oil in twenty minutes, stop boring!).

So, as a speaker, you're constantly adjusting your speech to the audience's reaction.

Speaking creates an energy not present in the written word. Reading a book or an article is a solitary experience. But when you are surrounded by hundreds of other people, reacting to the message, there is an energy and excitement.

And, one theory of persuasion argues that we don't know what we think until we sense the reactions of those around us. That doesn't happen with reading.

Critique groups, then, are essential. You have to solicit feedback *before* you publish from writing groups. (Make sure it's a critique group and not a "Say something nice about me, and I'll say something nice about you" group!)

Focus groups are another important tool. When I worked with teen curriculum, we would bring in actual teachers and students to critique the curriculum before we ever went to press.

When I was a freelancer, I hired my daughter and her friends to go over every word of every book. The fifty bucks I paid them well worth it!

"You really don't want to use that word?"

"Why?"

"Well, it, ah, it doesn't mean what you think it means to teens today."

Editors are our friends. Let's say that together, boys and girls. "Editors are our friends."

While editorial director of teen curriculum, I would tell the editor—who worked for *me*—"Treat my article like you would any other manuscript." Patsy was a former English teacher with a red pen. My manuscript would look like the "St. Valentine Day Massacre" when she got done, but it was always better.

To paraphrase Abraham Lincoln, "The person who is his own editor, has a fool for a client."

So, in writing, your audience is unseen, but it's not un-knowable.

On the stage, it's live and improvised; on the page it's carefully scripted and edited.

That's why I'd rather be writing than speaking. With speaking, it's like the Olympics. No matter how much practice you've put into the talk inevitably there will be glitches: you lose your place, your train of thought derails, a child falls out of the balcony (it turned out to be a doll, but I really lost my timing), you don't stick your landing.

In print, everything is in your control, and if you don't catch a *faux pas*, hopefully the editor will. In fact, I prefer doing email interviews. I can carefully think through the question, choose my words, and let it sit a day or two to make sure that's what I really want to say. I get in trouble when I ad lib! And I'm ADD, so I can get very distracted, which is—what was I saying? oh yes— why my notes are in manuscript form. So writing is a controlled, safe environment.

On the stage, you can use 4,500 words; on the page 1,500. A half hour talk will use up about 4,500 words speaking at 150 words per minute. In an article or a book chapter slash that by one-third. You've got to "write tight"!

On the stage, you may speak to a thousand people; on the page, you can easily reach *100* thousand.

Speaking may be the most effective mode of persuasion, but it's not the most efficient.

For instance, I recently spoke to one hundred people at a seminar. I spent a day working on the talk and then one day at the nearby conference center delivering it. So, my ratio of impact was fifty people per day.

That same week, I spent a day writing an article for *Decision* magazine which reaches 1.8 million readers. To reach that many people at one hundred people at a time, I would have to speak 18,000 days in a row or for 4,931 years! My ratio of impact was exponentially greater.

And there is the advantage that the talk is somewhat permanent when put into print. Every so often I'll get an email telling how the writer was helped by the article they just read. They must have read it in a waiting room or were cleaning out their magazine rack because I wrote in ten years ago! Online writing is even better since it's available indefinitely, long after the magazine is in the recycle bin, to a worldwide audience.

The New Testament implies that Apollos was a much better speaker than the apostle Paul. And during the time of the famous preacher Charles Spurgeon, another pastor in London was actually considered a better preacher. So why do we know the names of Paul and Spurgeon over Apollos and "another pastor"? They both wrote! Paul penned nearly half the New Testament and Spurgeon published his weekly sermons as well as a monthly magazine.

Writing is a personal, intimate, one-on-one "conversation." From your perspective in the audience, the speaker on stage is speaking to you—and a thousand other people. But on the page, the author is speaking directly to you. You've got Dave Barry all to yourself!

As I mentioned, a judge in a *Campus Life* "Book of the Year" contest wrote, "Jim Watkins is not an author. No, it's like he's sitting across from you at McDonald's sharing Diet Cokes."

That's personal.

Writing takes place at *your* time and space. You set the time and place, as well as the pace. Unlike other forms of mass communication—even audio books—you can read as slowly or quickly as you like. You can easily go back and re-read a section that isn't clear. And, you can highlight, underline, dog ear and make notes in the margins in a magazine or book. (Try doing that with your Kindle!).

While the stage and page are two very different venues, there are lots of similarities.

The stage and page both require a great introduction

A good lead attracts attention. Think of it as those screaming announcers on car commercials. "AT CRAZY CARL'S CAR CORRAL, WE'LL PUT YOU IN A BRAND NEW CAR WITH NO MONEY DOWN, NO PAYMENTS FOR THREE MONTHS. PLUS. . . ."

A good lead establishes the subject. Within a few seconds, your audience should know the exact subject.

A good lead sets the tone. Remember, this book is about writing with banana peels, so your lead has got to be humorous.

A good lead doesn't make promises it can't keep. Back to our car commercial. You know very well there's some kind of catch or a disclaimer at the end of the commercial read at five hundred words per minute: "Some restrictions apply based on credit rating and inventory availability. Does not include dealer prep and destination charges. Not valid on sunny days or even-numbered dates. . . ."

If you don't fulfill the promises made in the lead or introduction, your audience will feel just as deceived.

You can certainly build anticipation by withholding key points or ideas until later in the message, but make sure you deliver later.

Leads can include:

A humorous anecdote

A shocking or silly statement

A question that addresses a felt need:

"Do you ever feel alone in a church of two thousand?"

"When was the last time you and your spouse had some time away?"

"Do you want to write with humor?"

A memory-inducing anecdote. Just be sure you know your audience and that it's a memory that they can recall.

"Do you remember where you were when John F. Kennedy was assassinated?" will only work for aging "baby-boomers."

Jumping right into the middle of the action. Don't spend half a page clearing throat.

Conversation. An article on the intrinsic differences between males and females was starting to read like a term paper, so I transferred the information into a Sunday school class discussion. The article began with the student trying to stump the teacher with a difficult question. Various students added their opinions and questions. Suddenly, the potentially academic article became a lively interchange of information and humor.

Use universal illustrations

In local setting, you can use, well, local settings. In writing for an international audience, avoid your local context. For instance, in some countries, dog aren't pets—they're entrees.

Your tool box may be lighter when you write, but it's not empty.

14

'I'm out of ideas—
and I'm up against a deadline!'

There's nothing to writing.
All you do is sit down at a typewriter and open a vein.
Walter "Red" Smith

Brainstorming topics and titles

Every week for fifteen years, I stared at a blank computer screen—the cursor taunting me—praying that an idea for my weekly newspaper column would magically appear. The deadline for the three newspapers was Thursday at noon. And nearly half the time, I'd crawl out of bed at 6 AM, steel myself with a handful of dark chocolate and numerous cans of Diet Coke—and not have a single idea for the column.

I'd watch the morning news programs. Nothing! Scan my favorite news and views Internet sites. Nothing! Eat some more dark chocolate. Nothing! One morning, it was T-minus two hours and counting—and still nothing. So, in utter desperation, I wrote:

Top ten column-writing secrets revealed

Writing a weekly column isn't exactly like creating something that high school students will be required to read 100 years from now. It is, however, a challenge coming up with a fresh, insightful essay every seven days—or at least some ink spots to fill 15 inches of column space.

So, I have in my right hand, direct from my home office, today's top ten list: Top Ten Column Writing Secrets.

10. **Eat cold pizza for breakfast**

Wash it down with large quantities of Diet Coke. After three cans, I can type 470 words per minute but unfortuwythdly nonr ofit makerigh anv senze aftcher tke thirdddddddd . . .

9. **Travel**

I had great fun filing these columns from India ("The Land without Toilet Paper"), as well as southern Africa and the Caribbean.

But some of my best ideas have come while stuck in traffic in downtown Chicago in August with a stick shift with no air-conditioning and two kids in the backseat waging a fight to the death.

And, of course, anytime I fly, I always come back with new column ideas. You can read "Top Ten Things *Not* to Say at Security" at www.jameswatkins.com.

8. **Get married, have kids**

Dave Barry provides positive proof that marriage and raising children is a source for hundreds of columns, thousands of dollars, and even a Pulitzer Prize. However, he's also on his third or fourth marriage and is buying baby diapers with his AARP discount card.

That's why you won't find Lois mentioned in many of my columns. I love my wife and I want to stay married to her.

Kids, on the other hand, provide a great—and printable—source of humor. (You can read all about them at www.jameswatkins.com)

7. Read

Read everything: fortune cookies, warning labels, airline magazines, junk mail, movie credits, etc. etc.

Recently, I was waiting in the foyer of a restaurant and noticed a marker board sign that should have read PLEASE WAIT TO BE SEATED. Someone had erased the second S, making me wonder if *I* was going to be on the menu.

The best comedy, however, comes from the Department of Political-Correctness. After reading about Native Americans being offended by use of "Redskins" and other "Indian" terms in sports, I got thinking, where will this end? Is my state going to be forced to change its name to "Native Americana"?

6. Pass a kidney stone

I keep reminding students at writers' conferences, "nothing terrible happens to authors, just terrific anecdotes."

So, when I experienced the sensation of having a Greyhound bus overloaded with passengers on their way to a Weight Watchers convention parked on my lower back, I knew I had a great column. You can read it all about it at www.jameswatkins.com.

5. Tackle a home-improvement project

For example, I don't believe in paying a repair technician $50 per hour when I can fix it myself. What do I have to lose? It's already broken, so I really can't do too much more damage.

Such was the case with the "simple"—watch out for that word—task of removing the bathroom stool so the tile crew could install new floor covering. And I'd save $50 by doing it myself!

Eventually I had to bring the City Water Department in on the project, but it did make a great story which has appeared in several magazines and in a book. You can read about it at www.jameswatkins.com.

4. Use your column for shameless self-promotion

I'm not above using excerpts from my 14 books for columns, and then shamelessly mentioning that they are available at my online bookstore at www.jameswatkins.com. And if you have a Web site with your best (?) columns archived, you can make references to it through out the entire column.

3. Don't be afraid of people thinking you're crazy

Henri Nouwen writes of the successful communicator:

"He does not allow anybody to worship idols, and he constantly invites his fellow man to ask real, often painful and upsetting questions, to look behind the surface of smooth behavior, and take away all obstacles that prevent him from getting to the heart of the matter. The contemplative critic takes away the illusionary mask of the manipulative world and has the courage to show what the true situation is. He knows that he is considered by many as a fool, a madman, a danger to society, and a threat to mankind."

2. Have a friend who is even crazier than you

I enjoy having lunch with a fellow columnist who wishes to remain anonymous (I'll call him "Michael Fraley"). Michael describes his mind as "a box of kittens" and he never ceases to get my brain cells firing on all neurons. Most of our brainstorms, however, aren't fit for print such as his low-tech terrorist "Amish bin Laden"!

1. Create a top ten List

If all else fails, simply slap together a list such as, oh say, "Top ten column-writing secrets revealed." (And, of course, top ten lists can be found at

Okay, you can only go to that well once in your column-writing career, so, here are some questions I've developed to try to jump start ideas:

What if questions . . .

Qualities
What if it were bigger? smaller?
What if it were a different color? shape?
What if it were upside down? inside out?
What if it were younger? older?
What if it were faster? slower?
What if it were lighter? heavier?
What if it visible? invisible?
What if it were edible? inedible?
What if it were easy? hard?
What if it were animate? inanimate?
What if it were movable? immovable?
What if it could talk? was mute?
What if it were male? female? asexual?
What if it evil? righteous?
What if it were the exact opposite?
What if it ran in reverse?

Uses
What if it were used for something other than its intended usage?
What if it came with instructions? without instructions?
What if it were high tech? low tech?
What if the government took it over?
What if it were regulated? unregulated?
What if it were free? sold?
What if it were taken to the extreme?

What if it were made into a TV show? a song?

Other
What if it were combined with X?
What if it had never been invented?
What if it were in the future? in the past?

Atomic-powered idea generator

And once you've produced this literary work of art, what are
you going to title it.

I start with the subject in a circle in the middle of a blank
page then start adding circles for synonyms, antonyms,

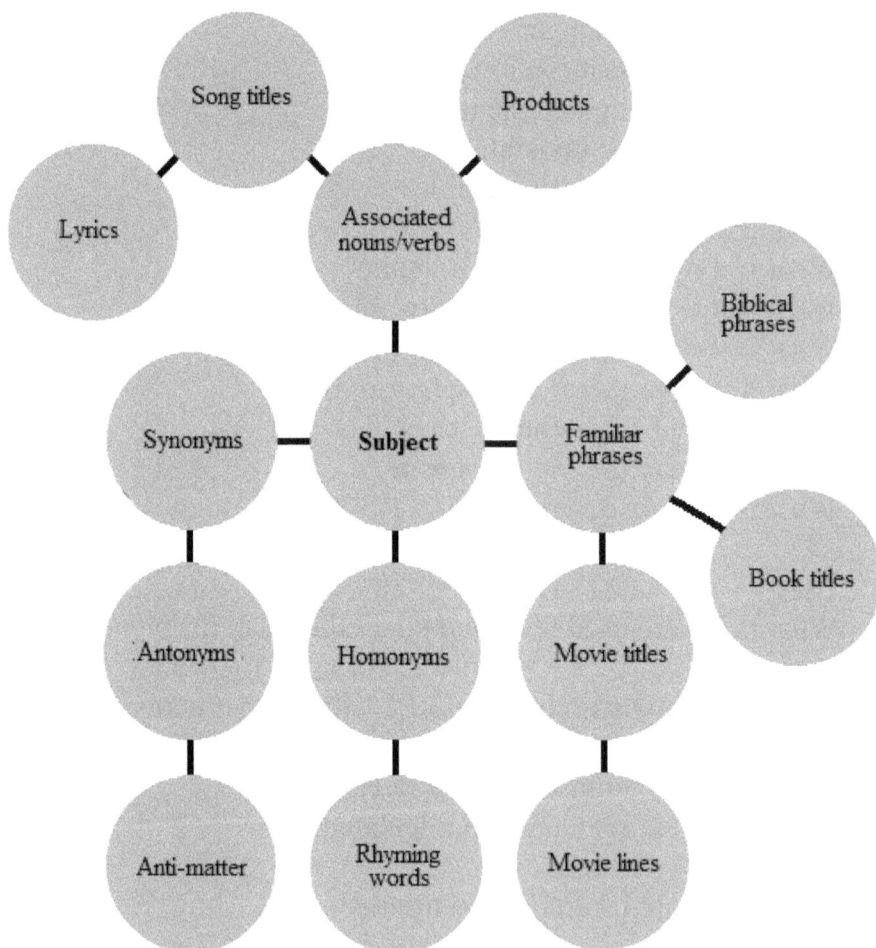

homonyms, rhyming words, associated nouns and verbs, biblical phrases, etc.

Let the atomic reaction begin!

Keep brainstorming until fission has slowed down, then start looking for relationships between the various circles. For instance, I was asked to write an article for a funeral director on the importance of showing emotion. I wrote GRIEF in the middle circle and fission-ed out to topics such as EMOTIONS, FEELING; FUNERAL HOME, CEMETARY, BURIAL PLOT; etc. Then I made the connection between FEELINGS and BURIAL and came up with "Don't bury your feelings."

Here are some of my favorite titles that came out of this atomic reaction:

Synonyms on a lack of follow-up in most evangelism efforts: "Losing the found" (Word pair)

Antonyms on faith healing: "Healing: faith or fake?"

Homonyms on cult abuse: "Sects and violence"

Rhyming words on some Christians' unhealthy emphases on demon activity: "Demons: possession or obsession?"

Associated nouns and verbs on importance of talking about grief at a funeral: "Don't bury your feelings"

Familiar phrases, titles on the importance of encouragement: "Affirmative Action;" on the message of Christmas: "The *365 Days* of Christmas"

Book titles: Articles called "The Purpose-Driven Writer," "The Papoose-Driven Life"

Most of all, have fun and let the reaction begin.

15

Do no harm

Humor is a rubber sword—it allows you to make a point without drawing blood.
Mary Hirsch

Use humor to help, not hurt
Most late-night and Internet humor seems to be—at least to *moi*—rude, crude, and lewd. While Christ used irony, satire, paradox, and hyperbole, we find only one case of sarcasm: Matthew 23.

So, let me suggest humorist follow the Hippocratic Oath: Do no harm.

That's why you won't find any examples of obscene, racist, sexist humor in this book. It takes no [bleeping] effort or [bleeping] creativity to make fun of [bleeping] [bleeps], [bleep] it!

Use humor to introduce or reinforce a point
Humor used simply to get the reader's attention—or to keep them awake between points nine and ten—merely distracts from the point we're trying to make.

Ideally, when readers remember the humor, they remember the message.

Use humor discreetly, tastefully
Know your audience's sensitivities. And never, ever, use

ethnic, racist, or sexist humor. This doesn't mean you can't use humor with sensitive subjects (remember my humorous intros for my book on *death.*).

Use humor sparingly

As a teen I decided to help make spaghetti sauce while my mom was in the hospital. I carefully added the tomato paste and tomato sauce and the one-quarter cup of garlic.

I'm not exactly "Mr. Food," so I didn't realize the recipe called for *chopped* garlic. I poured in a quarter cup of *powered* garlic. My family had bad breath for two weeks!

So, treat humor like your would *powered* garlic. Gingerly season (pun intended) your manuscript with humor.

16

How to recoup the cost of this book

A man's got to take a lot of punishment to
write a really funny book.
Ernest Hemingway

Just in case your parents are still wondering why you're spending *their* money for you to take a class on *humor* writing or you're wondering if you'll every recoup the cost of this book, here's the good news. I guarantee, that if you'll follow the principles in this book, you can make $13.99 with your humor writing.

From the 2009 *Writers' Market,* here's what you can expect.

Speech writing
$40-150 per hour for writing it (average: $90)
or $100-300 per minute of actual speech (average: $200)

Joke-writing services, stand-up material
$5-50 per joke
Most stand ups pay $25-50 per joke (one-liners less, stories more)

TV comic monologues, radio DJ material, and stand-up routines need thousands of jokes daily. Someone described the market as a "joke-eating shark" hungry for chum, although I'd like to think of my writing as more than a bucket of fish guts.

Radio commercials
$30-85 per hour for writing it
or $120-850 per minute of air time (average: $500)

TV commercials
$60-80 per hour for writing it
or $150-2,500 per 30 seconds of air time (average: $1,000)

Greeting cards
$50-300 per idea

Cartoon gag lines
$30

Newspaper columns
$70-600 (average: $170)

Fillers
$5 and up
Readers Digest pays $100-300 for jokes, funny anecdotes—
and 80 million readers!

Letters to the editor
Zero! But here's the good news. Editors are starving for well-written, articulate, non-libelous letters. So, I started sending in well-written, articulate, non-libelous letters with lots of humor to my local paper.

You can reach hundreds of thousands of readers with a letter to the editor. (I actually had a letter to the editor printed in *TIME.*)

One day the local editor called and said, "Jim, could you please stop writing all these letters to the editor and just write a column every week?" That led to writing a weekly column for fifteen years.

Blogs

Zero! Zip! Zilch—with a few notable exceptions

The blog, "Stuff White People Like," was sold to Random House for $350,000!

"Postcards from Yo Momma" posted by Doree Shafrir and Jessica Grose featured user-submitted emails from "real moms." It became a hardcover book from Hyperion

The "White Trash Mom," a blog by Michelle Lamar, is now *White Trash Mom Handbook* from St. Martin's Press.

Okay, you may not make $350,000, but one afternoon an editor from Mulnomah Publishers called. "We saw the song you wrote for your daughter's graduation and we'd like to use it in our upcoming gift book."

It is a wonderful way to showcase your work and reach a potential audience of *billions*!

Two notes of warning:

1. Always put your copyright notice on all your online work. Yah, yah, most people think if it's online it's public domain. Not true! All the national and international laws apply to online material.

2. I only put previously published work on my site—except for my short rants on time-sensitive topics. Some publishers consider online material as "previously published" and will pay the cheaper reprint rights rather than the better paying first rights.

Sit-coms

$35-150 per hour for writing it or $800-1,000 per day

Know the biz

Sit-down comics face their own version of a "tough room"— the publication board!

You can never eliminate all rejection slips, but you can drastically reduce the virtual flying fruit by knowing the markets.

Writers' Market (Writers Digest Books) provides a catalog of what book publishers, periodicals, and online markets are paying humor—and the specific genre they are seeking.

The Christian Writers' Market Guide (Waterbrook) provides the Christian market offerings.

Follow the guidelines *exactly* and be persistent.

Going to writers' conferences is also essential for the serious writer. The University of Dayton sponsors the Erma Bombeck Writers' Workshop each spring. (Details at www.humorwriters.org.) Plus there are literally hundreds of writers' conferences across North America and the world. I've listed some of my favs at www.jameswatkins.com/manu.htm.

And it *is* a biz, believers

First, realize professional writing *is* a business.

For people of faith, that's hard to comprehend. The gospel may be *free*, but the cost of publication is *ungodly*. If a "ministry" can't pay the costs of paper, personnel, and promotion it's not going to be in ministry for long.

Christian publishers constantly struggle with what *needs* to be published and what will *sell* and keep them in ministry. Unfortunately, that's why Christian book stores—excuse me, Family Christian stores—are giving more and more shelf space to "Jesus junk" (T-shirts, Frisbees, cheesy art, and posters) and less and less to *books.* And that's why a lot of Christian books are pure fluff: McMessages that are tasty, but have 0 percent nutritional value.

It's not *what* you know, but *who* you know

There are three secrets to being published:

1. Networking
2. Networking and
3. Networking

Two quick examples.

I had tried for years to get published by a large general magazine. The editor came up to me at the Mount Hermon Christian Writers' Conference and said, "Jim, I love your writing. Why don't you send me something?"

I stammered, "Uh, I have, but you keep sending my

articles back."

"Well, you know me now. Send them again."

Within a year I was being *assigned* cover articles, features and book reviews.

Later that same year, an editor from one of the major Christian publishers came up to me at the Florida Christian Writers' Conference.

"Jim, I love your writing. Why don't you send me something?"

Again I stammered, "Uh, I have, but you keep sending my proposals back."

"Well, you know me now. Send them again."

Before I knew it, I had three of my own books and two anthologies with the publisher.

Here's the point. If you want to be published, you've got to meet editors face to face. All my carefully and cleverly constructed books proposals were getting the usual "Does not meet our editorial needs at this time" responses. *Until,* I started meeting editors.

So don't waste your time and money with manuscript submission services. Take that money and go to a conference with lots of editors who are looking for what you write. (And don't waste your time and money on conferences without lots of editors and agents.)

Do your research. Know the publishing houses "editorial needs at this time." And get in their faces!

Finally, there's self-publishing

Many best-selling books began as self-published books: *The Living Bible, The Shack, The Christmas Box,* etc. Most often, royalty publishers didn't see a ready market. "A paraphrased Bible?! There's no market for a paraphrased Bible!" Forty million copies later, *The Living Bible* is doing quite well.

Here are three questions to ask before self-publishing:

1. **Has a royalty publisher praised your book, but said there isn't a large enough market for them to publish it?**

2. **Do you have a way to reach that market?**

3. **Do you have the ability to produce it professionally?**
Can you afford to go with a reputable self-publisher that will produce a professional-looking product or do you have access to design and typography expertise to do it yourself. (A poor cover and interior design will cripple your sales. It must be able to compete with mainstream publishers.)

Self-publishing is a wonderful way to reach a narrow market (and become a big fish in a small pond) or to prove to royalty publishers that there is indeed a market for your work in the larger pond

The book that you're holding is self-published because the market for Christian humor writers is roughly the size as the market for underwater ukulele players. But, because I speak at ten or so writers' conferences a year—and force my "Humor Writing" students to buy it as a required text book—it's doing well.

Unfortunately, there are a *lot* of self-publishing scams out there, so please read my warnings at www.jameswatkins.com/selfpublishing.htm before you sign a contract.

If you follow my advice, I can guarantee you that you'll recoup the $13.99 you spent for this book. Maybe more!

James N. Watkins

Jim is the award-winning author of fifteen books and over two thousand articles including fifteen years as a humor columnist for three newspapers.

He serves as an editor with Wesleyan Publishing House and instructor at Taylor University, as well as popular conference speaker. His most important roles, however, are as a child of God, husband, dad, and "papaw."

His books include:

Squeezing Good Out of Bad (XarisCom, 2009)

Communicate to Change Lives (Wesleyan Publishing House, 2007)

Writers on Writing (Wesleyan Publishing House, 2005)

The Why Files (Three-book series, Concordia 2000)

Characters: Comedy and Drama (Lillenas, 1993)

Order one—or the whole bunch—at www.jameswatkins.com.

XarisCom

XarisCom's mission is "to communicate the gospel of Christ in as creative manner as possible with as many people as possible."

It fulfills its mission through print and online publishing. It has been recognized by the Billy Graham Evangelistic Association and Gospel.com for its creative approach to sharing the gospel. *Creator* magazine describes its products as "humorous and witty . . . edifying the Body and glorifying God in an entertaining way."

Learn how you can support this ministry at www.xariscom.com.

*So there ain't nothing more to write about, and I am rotten glad
of it, because if I'd a knowed what a trouble it was to make a
book I wouldn't a tackled it, and ain't a-going to no more.*
Tom Sawyer in *The Adventures of Huckleberry Finn*

www.ingramcontent.com/pod-product-compliance
Lightning Source LLC
Chambersburg PA
CBHW031853090426
42741CB00005B/476